Journey to Confidence

Discovering the Self-Esteem Roadmap to Your Best Self

Michelle Mann

Contents

Chapter One

Journey to Confidence

Discovering the Self-Esteem Roadmap to Your Best Self

In a world that often feels like it's constantly evaluating us, confidence can be our most treasured asset. It's that inner voice that whispers, "You've got this," even when the odds seem stacked against us. But what is confidence, really? It's more than just feeling good about ourselves. It's a deep-rooted belief in our worth and abilities, a precious psychological resource that can lead us to achieve great things, foster meaningful relationships, and find genuine satisfaction in life.

Imagine for a moment a life where you're constantly second-guessing yourself, where every decision feels like a mountain to climb. That's the life of someone with low self-esteem. Such individuals often find themselves trapped in a cycle of self-doubt, depression, and even tolerating abusive situations. On the flip side, an inflated sense of self can lead to entitlement, an inability to learn from mistakes, and even narcissistic tendencies. Finding the right balance is crucial.

But here's the good news: self-esteem isn't set in stone. It's a journey, not a destination. Our self-worth can ebb and flow based on our experiences, both good and bad. From childhood memories to adult relationships, various factors can shape how we view ourselves. Yet, with the right tools and mindset, we can navigate these challenges and emerge stronger.

This book, "Journey to Confidence: Discovering the Self-Esteem Roadmap to Your Best Self," is your guide on this transformative journey. We'll delve deep into the intricacies of self-esteem, exploring its origins, its impact on our lives, and most importantly, how to nurture and grow it. Drawing from up-to-date research and real-life stories, we'll uncover strategies to boost your self-worth, overcome setbacks, and embrace your true self.

In the chapters that follow, we'll also dive into the societal pressures that often shape our self-perception. The digital age, with its relentless barrage of 'perfect' images and lifestyles, can sometimes skew our understanding of self-worth. But by grounding ourselves in authenticity and self-awareness, we can rise above these external pressures. We'll explore exercises, anecdotes, and actionable steps to help you reclaim your confidence and redefine your self-image in a positive, empowering light.

As we navigate this journey, it's essential to remember that confidence isn't just about how we see ourselves, but also how we interact with the world around us. It's the courage to voice our opinions, the resilience to bounce back from failures, and the humility to acknowledge and learn from our mistakes. In this digital era, where comparisons are just a click away, it's easy to feel lost in the crowd. But true confidence stems from recognizing and celebrating our unique strengths, passions, and experiences. This book will not only guide you in understanding the core of your self-worth but also equip you with tools to shine brightly in your authentic light, amidst the noise and chaos of the modern world. Embrace this journey with an open heart, and witness the transformative power of genuine self-confidence.

Remember, each one of us is unique, and our worth isn't determined by external factors. It's an intrinsic part of who we are. So, whether you're someone struggling with self-doubt or someone looking to further enhance your self-belief, this book is for you. Let's embark on this journey together and discover the roadmap to your best self.

Welcome to a journey of self-discovery, growth, and boundless confidence. Let's get started!

An Honest Recounting of a Personal Struggle with Confidence and Self-Esteem

Growing up, I was the kid who always sat at the back of the class, hoping not to be noticed. My voice, both literally and metaphorically, was but a whisper in a world that seemed to be constantly shouting. Every time I looked in the mirror, I saw a reflection of doubt, of someone who believed they were never quite "enough" - not smart enough, not attractive enough, not talented enough.

It began early, this feeling of inadequacy. I remember being in elementary school, watching my peers effortlessly answer questions, participate in sports, or even just engage in simple conversations. While they soared, I felt anchored by a weight of self-doubt. Every mistake, no matter how minor, felt like a confirmation of my deepest fears. Every success, on the other hand, felt like a fluke, a stroke of luck that wasn't truly deserved.

My teenage years only intensified these feelings. The world seemed to be divided into those who "had it" and those who didn't, and I firmly believed I fell into the latter category. Social media didn't help. Scrolling through feeds filled with picture-perfect moments, I constantly compared my behind-the-scenes with everyone else's highlight reel. It felt like everyone had figured life out, while I was still fumbling in the dark.

But the turning point came in my early twenties. After a particularly challenging day, a close friend sat me down and shared her own struggles with self-esteem. It was a revelation. Here was someone I had always seen as confident and accomplished, revealing her own insecurities and fears. That conversation was the beginning of my journey toward understanding that self-worth isn't something you're born with; it's something you build.

It wasn't an overnight transformation. It took therapy, introspection, and a lot of unlearning of deep-seated beliefs. But with time, I began to see myself not as a collection of flaws but as a unique individual with strengths and weaknesses, just like everyone else. I learned to celebrate small victories, embrace failures as learning opportunities, and most importantly, be kinder to myself.

Looking back, I realize that my struggle with confidence and self-esteem, though painful, has been a valuable teacher. It has taught me empathy, resilience, and the importance of self-acceptance. And while the journey is ongoing, I'm proud of how far I've come and excited for the road ahead.

The Connection Between Confidence and Self-Esteem

At first glance, confidence and self-esteem might seem like interchangeable terms. Both are associated with a positive self-view and are often touted as the keys to success and happiness. However, delve a little deeper, and you'll find that while they are closely intertwined, they are distinct concepts, each playing a unique role in our personal growth and well-being.

Self-esteem is the foundation. It's our internal assessment of our worth and value. Think of it as the bedrock upon which our self-image is built. It's the deep-seated belief that we are deserving of love, respect, and understanding, regardless of our achievements or external validations. When our self-esteem is healthy, we recognize our intrinsic worth, independent of external accolades or setbacks.

On the other hand, confidence is the outward manifestation of this inner belief. It's the courage to act based on our self-assessment. While self-esteem is about how we perceive ourselves, confidence is about how we present ourselves to the world. It's the voice that says, "I can do this," the stride with which we walk into a room, and the way we tackle challenges head-on.

Now, here's where the connection becomes crucial: our confidence is often a reflection of our self-esteem. When we genuinely believe in our worth and abilities, it shows in our actions. We take risks, voice our opinions, and embrace new opportunities, not because we are certain of success, but because we know that our value isn't solely defined by outcomes.

However, it's essential to understand that while self-esteem feeds confidence, the reverse is also true. Every time we step out of our comfort zone and succeed, it reinforces our self-belief. And even when we fail, if we've built a robust sense of self-worth, we see these setbacks not as reflections of our inadequacy but as opportunities to learn and grow.

In essence, self-esteem and confidence are two sides of the same coin. One is the internal belief in our worth, and the other is the external demonstration of that belief. Together, they form a virtuous cycle, each reinforcing and amplifying the other. As we journey through this book, we'll explore how to nurture both, understanding that a true sense of self-worth is incomplete without the courage to express and act on it.

Actionable Roadmap Readers Will Embark Upon

Embarking on a journey of self-discovery and growth is no small feat, and it's essential to have a clear roadmap to guide the way. This book is designed to be that guiding light, providing readers with a structured, actionable pathway to nurture both their self-esteem and confidence. Here's a glimpse of what you can expect as you turn the pages:

1. Self-Assessment: Before we can chart a course forward, we need to understand where we stand. The initial chapters will introduce tools and exercises to help you gauge your current levels of self-esteem and confidence. This isn't about judgment but about gaining clarity.

2. Understanding the Roots: We'll delve deep into the origins of self-worth, exploring childhood experiences, societal influences, and past traumas that might have shaped your self-perception. By understanding the past, we can better navigate the present and future.

3. Building a Strong Foundation: With a clear understanding of our starting point, we'll focus on strengthening the bedrock of self-esteem. Through guided exercises, personal anecdotes, and expert insights, you'll learn to cultivate a genuine appreciation for yourself, flaws, and all.

4. Taking Action: With a fortified sense of self-worth, we'll transition into boosting confidence. This section will be packed with practical steps to help you step out of your comfort zone, from public speaking tips to strategies for handling criticism with grace.

5. Maintaining Momentum: Growth is a continuous journey. We'll explore techniques to keep the momentum going, ensuring that the progress you make is sustainable. This includes building resilience, practicing self-compassion, and continuously challenging yourself.

6. Creating a Supportive Environment: While much of the journey is internal, external factors play a significant role. We'll discuss how to surround yourself with positive influences, set boundaries, and seek support when needed.

7. Celebrating Milestones: Every step forward, no matter how small, is a victory. We'll emphasize the importance of recognizing and celebrating these milestones, reinforcing the positive changes you're making.

As you journey through this roadmap, remember that it's not about perfection but progress. Each chapter is designed to be both informative and actionable, ensuring that you're not just reading about change but actively participating in it. By the end, you'll have a toolkit of strategies, insights, and exercises to help you navigate the world with a renewed sense of self-worth and confidence. Let's embark on this transformative journey together!

Chapter Two

Understanding the Origin of Self-Doubt

"The worst enemy to creativity is self-doubt." – Sylvia Plath

Every journey begins with understanding the starting point. Before we can truly build upon our self-esteem and confidence, it's essential to delve into the roots of our self-doubt. Where do these nagging feelings of inadequacy come from? Why do certain situations trigger a spiral of negative self-talk? This chapter aims to shed light on these questions.

Self-doubt isn't something we're born with; it's cultivated over time through a myriad of experiences, interactions, and influences. From early childhood memories to recent setbacks, various factors shape our perception of ourselves and our abilities. By tracing back to these origins, we can gain a clearer understanding of our current mindset and, more importantly, identify ways to challenge and change these deep seated beliefs.

In this chapter, we'll explore the psychological, societal, and personal events that contribute to self-doubt. We'll also touch upon the evolutionary and biological aspects of self-doubt, offering a holistic view of this complex emotion. Through introspective exercises, real-life anecdotes, and expert insights, we'll embark on a journey of self-awareness, setting the stage for the transformative chapters ahead.

So, let's dive deep, unravel the tapestry of our past, and uncover the seeds of self-doubt. Only by understanding its origins can we truly begin the process of healing and growth.

Sub-chapter 1.1: The Psychological Roots of Self-Doubt

The Early Influencers: Parental, Societal, and Peer Pressures

From the moment we're born, we're shaped by the world around us. Our first teachers, our parents, play a pivotal role in molding our self-perception. Their praises, criticisms, and even the subtle cues they might not be aware of can deeply influence how we view ourselves. Were you constantly compared to a sibling or a neighbor's child? Were your achievements celebrated, or were they overshadowed by what you 'could have done better'? These early interactions lay the groundwork for our self-worth.

As we grow, society and peers join the mix. The playground can be both a place of joy and a battleground where our self-worth is tested. Remember the first time you felt left out of a game or were picked last for a team? These experiences, though seemingly trivial, can plant seeds of self-doubt that sprout over time.

In today's digital age, societal pressures have taken a new form. Social media platforms bombard us with images of 'perfect' lives, setting unrealistic standards. Every scroll, every like, every comment can either boost our confidence or chip away at our self-esteem.

But it's not just about external pressures. Our internal dialogue, often shaped by these early influencers, plays a crucial role. How many times have you held yourself back, thinking you're not good enough? These self-limiting beliefs, often rooted in childhood experiences and societal norms, can become our biggest barriers.

In this section, we'll delve deep into these early influencers, understanding their impact and learning how to navigate their lasting effects. By recognizing and addressing these foundational experiences, we can start rewriting our narrative, one where self-doubt is replaced with self-assurance.

The Role of Past Failures and Traumas

Life is a tapestry of experiences, and while many of them are uplifting, others can leave scars that shape our self-perception for years to come. Past failures and traumas, whether big or small, can play a significant role in the development of self-doubt. Let's dive into this a bit deeper.

Think back to a time when you gave something your all, only to fall short. Maybe it was a project at work, a relationship, or even a personal goal. The sting of failure, especially when it's unexpected, can be a heavy blow to our confidence. Over time, if these failures aren't processed healthily, they can accumulate, leading us to question our abilities and worth.

Traumas, on the other hand, can be even more insidious. Experiences of bullying, emotional or physical abuse, or any form of trauma can deeply embed feelings of inadequacy and self-doubt. These events can create a narrative in our minds that we are somehow 'less than' or undeserving.

But here's the silver lining: understanding the role of these past experiences in shaping our self-doubt is the first step towards healing. By acknowledging and confronting these shadows, we can begin to rewrite our stories. In the upcoming sections, we'll explore strategies to process past failures and traumas, ensuring they become stepping stones, not stumbling blocks, on our journey to self-assuredness. Remember, it's not about erasing the past, but about learning, growing, and moving forward with newfound wisdom.

Genetic and Biological Factors

Alright, let's dive into the fascinating world of genetics and biology and see how they play a role in self-doubt.

Ever wondered why some people seem naturally confident while others struggle with self-doubt? Well, it's not just about upbringing or experiences; our genes play a part too. Recent studies have shown that self-esteem has a genetic component. A study conducted on Finnish twins born between 1983 and 1987 revealed some intriguing findings. The heritability of self-esteem was found to be different between boys and girls at different ages. For instance, at age 14, it was 0.62 for boys and 0.40 for girls. By age 17, these numbers changed to 0.48 for boys and 0.29 for girls. This suggests that genetics plays a more significant role in boys' self-esteem during early adolescence.

But it's not just about genes alone. The environment interacts with these genetic factors, influencing our self-worth. While genetics set the stage, our experiences, upbringing, and environment play their parts in the grand performance of our lives.

Interestingly, self-esteem doesn't remain constant throughout our lives. It evolves, showing patterns of stability and change during adolescence. Factors like family interactions, which were once considered the primary source of self-esteem development, are now seen in tandem with genetic factors. Some studies have even challenged the traditional view, emphasizing the significant role of genetics in self-esteem.

Now, while it's tempting to think, "Oh, it's in my genes, so there's nothing I can do," that's not entirely true. Remember, genes set the potential, but it's our environment and choices that determine how this potential is realized. So, even if you feel that self-doubt is in your DNA, there's always room for growth, change, and self-improvement. After all, we're all a mix of our genes, our experiences, and the choices we make. So, let's embrace the journey of understanding ourselves better, shall we?

Sub-chapter 1.2: Cultural and Societal Influences

The Media's Portrayal of Success

In today's digital age, the media wields an unparalleled influence on our perceptions, beliefs, and values. One area where this influence is particularly evident is in its portrayal of success. The media, with its vast reach and power, has the ability to shape public opinion, create sentiments, and even craft realities. But how does it define success?

Traditionally, success was often linked to tangible achievements like career milestones or financial prosperity. However, in the era of social media, success is frequently equated with a well-curated Instagram page or a viral TikTok video. It's about visibility, likes, shares, and the illusion of a perfect life. This portrayal can be misleading, creating unrealistic standards and fostering feelings of inadequacy among those who don't fit this mold.

Moreover, the media often leans towards advocacy journalism, where the objective is to persuade audiences into a particular narrative, rather than providing a holistic picture. This selective representation can skew our understanding of success, making it seem exclusive and unattainable.

But it's crucial to remember that success is deeply personal and subjective. While the media's portrayal can offer a glimpse into popular perceptions, true success lies in individual fulfillment, growth, and the pursuit of one's passions. As we navigate this chapter, we'll delve deeper into the media's influence, equipping you with the tools to discern, challenge, and redefine success on your own terms.

Peer Comparison on

Social Media

Ah, social media. A digital realm where we can connect, share, and sometimes, unfortunately, compare. We've all been there, scrolling through our feeds, only to stumble upon a friend's post showcasing their latest achievement, vacation, or life milestone. And while we may genuinely be happy for them, there's this tiny voice in the back of our minds that whispers, "Why isn't that me?"

Social media platforms, from Facebook to Instagram, have become deeply ingrained in our culture, especially among younger generations. But as we dive deeper into this digital world, we're beginning to see the psychological implications of constant exposure to others' highlight reels. One of the most significant effects? The phenomenon of peer comparison.

Social comparison isn't new. It's a natural human tendency to gauge our worth by sizing ourselves up against others. However, social media amplifies this process tenfold. On these platforms, we're not just comparing ourselves to a handful of peers but to hundreds, even thousands, of online 'friends.' And more often than not, we're viewing their curated, best versions of themselves, leading to feelings of inadequacy and self-doubt.

Research has shown that frequent social comparisons on social media can lead to increased feelings of depression, anxiety, and loneliness. It's a cycle: we log on for connection, but the more we scroll, the more disconnected and discontented we feel. The vast array of 'perfect' lives on display can make our own seem lackluster in comparison.

But here's the thing: social media isn't real life. It's a filtered, edited, and often exaggerated version of it. Everyone has challenges, struggles, and mundane days, but these rarely make it to the feed. So, as we navigate this section, let's remember to take what we see with a grain of salt, focus on our own journey, and use social media as a tool for connection, not comparison.

Societal Standards and Stereotypes

In our interconnected world, societal standards and stereotypes play a significant role in shaping our perceptions and beliefs about different groups of people. Stereotypes are generalized beliefs about a particular category of people. They can be an expectation about a group's personality, appearance, ability, or preferences. While some stereotypes might hold a grain of truth, many are overgeneralized, inaccurate, and resistant to new information.

The media, including movies, TV shows, advertisements, and news outlets, often perpetuate these stereotypes, either intentionally or unintentionally. For instance, think about the portrayal of success in popular culture. Often, success is depicted in terms of material wealth, physical beauty, or power. These portrayals can create unrealistic standards that individuals feel pressured to achieve, leading to feelings of inadequacy or self-doubt when they don't measure up.

Moreover, societal standards are not just about success. They encompass a wide range of expectations related to gender roles, body image, career choices, and more. For instance, women might feel pressured to look a certain way based on the beauty standards promoted in magazines and on social media. Men, on the other hand, might feel the need to conform to standards of masculinity and strength.

But here's the thing: these societal standards and stereotypes are not fixed. They evolve over time, influenced by cultural shifts, social movements, and individual choices. As we become more aware of the negative impact of these standards, we can challenge and change them. By recognizing the power of media and societal influence, we can make conscious choices about the content we consume and the beliefs we adopt. In doing so, we can pave the way for a more inclusive and diverse understanding of success and self-worth.

Sub-chapter 1.3: Recognizing Your Personal Triggers

Keeping a doubt diary

Ever had those moments where your mind is a whirlwind of doubts? "Am I good enough?", "Did I make the right decision?", "What if I fail?". We've all been there. Enter the "doubt diary" – a safe space to pour out all those nagging thoughts.

Imagine having a chat with a non-judgmental friend who's all ears. That's what this diary is. By jotting down your doubts, you're not just venting; you're acknowledging them. And guess what? Once they're out of your head and on paper, they often seem less intimidating.

Now, you might wonder, "Why focus on the negatives?" Well, it's not about dwelling on them but understanding them. Over time, you'll start to see patterns. Maybe you doubt yourself every time you're about to take a big step. Recognizing this can help you prepare and even counter those feelings.

Plus, revisiting past entries can show you how many doubts never materialized or were unfounded. It's like a reality check, reminding you that while our brains are wired to anticipate the worst, it doesn't always come to pass.

In today's digital age, where everything seems to be out in the open, there's something therapeutic about keeping a private diary. It's just for you. No filters, no judgments. So, next time doubt clouds your mind, grab that diary. It's your personal rain-check against the storm of uncertainties.

Remember, it's okay to have doubts. But it's also essential to understand them, learn from them, and grow. Your doubt diary is your companion on this journey. Safe travels!

Reflecting on Past Experiences

Reflection is a powerful tool. It's like taking a trip down memory lane, but with a purpose. When it comes to self-doubt, our past experiences can be both the cause and the cure. Let's explore how.

Think about a time when you felt on top of the world. Maybe you aced a project, or perhaps you overcame a personal challenge. Now, remember a moment when things didn't go as planned. Both these experiences, the highs and the lows, have shaped your perception of yourself.

Manisha Singh, in her article "Unlocking Confidence: The Power of Reflecting on Past Successes," emphasizes the value of reflecting on past successes to foster learning, growth, and self-assurance. She suggests a structured approach to reflection, breaking down past experiences into components like actions taken, skills harnessed, and strategies that yielded results. By acknowledging the effort put into creating success and confronting obstacles faced, we strengthen our sense of agency.

But it's not just about the successes. The setbacks, the mistakes, the 'what ifs' – they all play a role. By reflecting on these experiences, we can identify patterns in our reactions and behaviors. Maybe you tend to doubt yourself when faced with unfamiliar situations. Or perhaps criticism triggers your self-doubt.

Keeping a 'reflection journal' can be a game-changer. By jotting down your thoughts, feelings, and insights from past experiences, you create a roadmap to understanding your triggers. Over time, you'll be better equipped to anticipate, address, and even leverage these triggers to your advantage.

Remember, the past is a treasure trove of lessons. By reflecting on it, we not only understand ourselves better but also pave the way for a future filled with confidence and self-belief. So, grab that journal, and let's start this introspective journey!

Identifying Patterns of Negative Thinking

We've all been there. Those moments when our minds spiral into a vortex of negative thoughts. "I can't do this," "I'm not good enough," "What if I fail?" These thoughts can be persistent, and if left unchecked, they can become deeply ingrained patterns that influence our behavior and self-perception.

Negative thinking patterns, often referred to as cognitive distortions, are irrational or biased ways of thinking about ourselves and the world around us. They can stem from past experiences, societal influences, or even our biological makeup. The tricky part? We often don't recognize them because they've become our default way of processing information.

For example, if you've faced rejection in the past, you might develop a pattern of "catastrophizing," where you automatically anticipate the worst possible outcome in similar situations. Or perhaps you tend to "overgeneralize," believing that one negative event means everything will always go wrong.

So, how do we break free from these patterns? Awareness is the first step. Start by paying close attention to your thoughts, especially when faced with challenges. Are there recurring themes or phrases? Jot them down. Over time, you'll begin to see patterns emerge.

Once you've identified these patterns, challenge them. Ask yourself: "Is this thought based on facts or assumptions? Are there alternative explanations? How would I advise a friend thinking this way?" By dissecting and questioning these thoughts, you can begin to reframe them into more positive, constructive beliefs.

Remember, our thoughts shape our reality. By identifying and addressing patterns of negative thinking, we can pave the way for a more confident, empowered self. It's like spring cleaning for the mind, making space for positivity and growth. Ready to sweep away those cobwebs?

Sub-chapter 1.4: The Physical Manifestations of Self-Doubt

The Stress Connection

Hey there, ever noticed how your body reacts when you're feeling doubtful or uncertain? It's not just in your head; it's in your body too. Let's talk about that stress connection.

Stress is our body's natural response to challenging situations. It's like an internal alarm system. When faced with self-doubt, this alarm often goes off, triggering the body's fight-or flight response. Your heart races, your breath quickens, and you might even feel a bit jittery. This is your body preparing to face a perceived threat, even if that threat is just a thought.

Now, a little stress now and then? Totally normal. It can even be beneficial, helping you stay alert and focused. But when self-doubt keeps that stress response activated non-stop? That's when things can get tricky. Chronic stress can lead to a host of physical issues, from headaches and insomnia to digestive problems and even a weakened immune system.

Here's a fun (or not-so-fun) fact: Chronic stress can also mess with your blood sugar levels, increasing the risk of type 2 diabetes. And let's not even get started on how it can impact our cardiovascular and respiratory systems.

But here's the silver lining: By recognizing and addressing the root causes of our self-doubt, we can manage this stress response. It's all about understanding the connection, tuning into our bodies, and taking proactive steps to keep that internal alarm in check. So, as we delve deeper into this topic, remember: Your body and mind are interconnected. By nurturing one, you're taking care of the other. Let's embark on this journey to holistic well-being together!

Body Language Cues

Hey, friend! Ever caught yourself slouching when you felt unsure? Or maybe you've noticed someone else avoiding eye contact when they're feeling a bit insecure? That's body language speaking volumes, even without a single word.

Our bodies have this fascinating way of mirroring our internal emotions. When we're filled with self-doubt, it often manifests in subtle (and sometimes not-so-subtle) physical cues. Let's dive into some of these, shall we?

For starters, our posture can be a dead giveaway. Standing tall with shoulders back exudes confidence. On the flip side, a hunched posture might hint at feelings of insecurity or a desire to go unnoticed. And then there's eye contact. Direct eye contact can show engagement and confidence. But if someone's eyes are darting away or they're avoiding your gaze, it might be a sign of discomfort or doubt.

Now, think about the hands. Ever seen someone fidgeting with their fingers when nervous? Or maybe clenching their fists when they're trying to muster up some courage? These are all body language cues signaling what's brewing inside.

But here's the thing: while these cues can provide insights, they're not definitive proof of what someone's feeling. Context matters. For instance, someone might avoid eye contact not because they're doubtful, but because it's a cultural norm for them. Or they might be slouching simply because of a bad chair and not because of low self-esteem.

The key takeaway? Body language is a powerful tool in understanding ourselves and others. But always pair it with empathy and understanding. After all, we're all on this journey together, navigating the complex world of emotions and expressions. So, next time you spot these cues in yourself or others, take a moment to reflect, understand, and support. Because sometimes, a simple gesture of reassurance can make all the difference.

Impact on Health and Wellness

Hey there! Let's chat about something we often overlook: the physical toll self-doubt can take on our bodies. It's not just a mental or emotional thing; it's physical too.

When we're constantly second-guessing ourselves, it creates a stress response in our bodies. And guess what? This stress can manifest in ways we might not immediately link to self-doubt. Ever had that nagging headache or trouble sleeping? Or maybe you've felt a bit off but couldn't pinpoint why? Stress might be the sneaky culprit behind it.

According to the Mayo Clinic, stress symptoms can impact our body, mood, and even behavior. From headaches, muscle tension, and stomach upsets to feelings of anxiety, restlessness, and mood swings. And if we don't address this stress? It can lead to more severe health issues like high blood pressure, heart disease, and even diabetes.

But here's the silver lining: recognizing the connection between self-doubt, stress, and these physical symptoms is the first step towards managing them. By understanding our triggers and working on our self-doubt, we can reduce this stress and its impact on our health.

So, the next time you're feeling a bit under the weather, take a moment to check in with yourself. Are you stressed? Is self-doubt playing a role? Remember, your body and mind are deeply connected. By taking care of one, you're looking out for the other. Let's prioritize our holistic well-being, one step at a time!

Sub-chapter 1.5: Countering First Impressions

The Power of Perception

Hey there! Let's chat about something we've all experienced: first impressions. You know, that split-second judgment we make when we meet someone or encounter something new? It's all about perception.

First impressions are powerful. As the saying goes, "You make only one first impression." Whether it's a colleague dressing sharply on the first day of class or the way someone carries themselves at a party, these initial moments can leave a lasting impact. But here's the twist: these impressions aren't always accurate.

According to an article on Psychology Today, the sequence in which we encounter information plays a significant role in how we judge subsequent details. This is linked to the "halo effect," where a positive quality in one aspect can influence our perception of other related qualities. For instance, meeting a friendly person might lead you to assume they're also generous, even if there's no direct correlation.

But while first impressions can set the tone, they don't always hold up in the long run. Substance ultimately has the final say. Think about it: if you only knew Einstein by his wild hair, you might have a different impression. But now, his face symbolizes genius.

The takeaway? While first impressions matter, it's essential to look beyond them. Dive deeper, challenge your perceptions, and be open to seeing the full picture. Because, in the end, it's the substance and genuine connections that truly count. Let's journey together in understanding the nuances of perception and its powerful impact on our lives!

Rewriting the Narrative

Have you ever heard a story about someone, formed an opinion, and then later discovered more details that completely changed your perspective? It's like watching a movie with a plot twist that makes you rethink the entire storyline. This is the essence of rewriting our narratives.

Imagine you've heard about a guy from the 1930s who seemed to be supporting the Nazis, and you instantly label him as a villain. But then, you find out he's Oskar Schindler, who secretly saved countless Jewish lives. Your entire perception shifts, right? That's the power of new information and reinterpretation.

Our brains are wired to form quick judgments based on limited information. It's a survival mechanism. But in today's complex world, first impressions can often be misleading. When we get new information that contradicts our initial beliefs, it can be challenging to change our implicit feelings, those gut reactions we have without conscious thought. However, when this new info forces us to reinterpret our previous understanding, our feelings can indeed shift.

So, what's the takeaway? Be open to rewriting your narratives. Just because you've always believed something doesn't mean it's the full story. New information can, and should, reshape our perceptions. After all, life is full of plot twists, and being adaptable in our thinking allows us to navigate them more effectively.

Using Doubt as a Motivator

Hey there! Let's chat about something that might surprise you: doubt can be a secret weapon. Yep, you read that right. While it's often seen as a negative emotion, when channeled correctly, doubt can be a powerful motivator.

According to a piece on TED Ideas, self-doubt, when managed properly, can combat complacency and enhance our preparation and performance. It pushes us to question outcomes, experiment with strategies, and be open to different problem-solving methods. This aligns perfectly with qualities like curiosity and resilience.

But here's the twist: self-doubt isn't just about boosting performance. It can also make us wiser leaders, teachers, parents, and friends. Embracing and understanding our self-doubt makes us more compassionate, offering deeper insights into ourselves and others.

The key to leveraging self-doubt lies in our core beliefs about ourselves, specifically in our "self-efficacy." This term, introduced by psychologist Albert Bandura, refers to our confidence in our ability to succeed in various endeavors. High self-efficacy is crucial because if we don't genuinely believe we can achieve the results we desire, we're less likely to even try.

But here's the golden nugget: while self-doubt is natural and everyone experiences it (even legends like Maya Angelou!), it's essential to see it as an opportunity for growth.

By understanding and harnessing self-doubt, we can transform it into a driving force for improvement and success.

So, next time doubt creeps in, remember: it's not a sign of weakness. It's a call to action, a nudge to push harder, and a reminder that growth often comes from challenging our beliefs and perceptions. Let's turn that doubt into drive and make magic happen!

Chapter Three

The Science Behind Self-Esteem

"What lies behind us and what lies before us are tiny matters compared to what lies within us." – Ralph Waldo Emerson

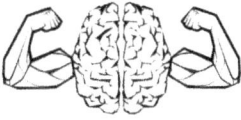

As we journey deeper into the realm of self-esteem, it's time to don our lab coats and delve into the fascinating science behind it. While our previous chapter explored the origins and manifestations of self-doubt, this chapter will illuminate the intricate workings of our brain and the psychological theories that underpin self-esteem.

Ever wondered why some people seem naturally confident while others grapple with self-worth? Or why certain experiences can drastically alter our self-perception? The answers lie in a blend of neuroscience, psychology, and even genetics. From the neurotransmitters playing a role in our self-perception to the psychological models that explain our self-worth, we're about to embark on a riveting exploration.

But don't worry, we'll keep the jargon to a minimum and ensure everything's easy to grasp. Think of this chapter as a friendly science class, where we unravel the mysteries of the mind and discover the building blocks of self-esteem. So, strap in and get ready for a deep dive into the captivating world of the science behind self-esteem. Let's uncover the magic that makes us who we are!

Sub-chapter 2.1: The Neurology of Confidence

Brain Regions Involved

Let's embark on a fascinating journey into the intricate maze of our brain and discover the regions that play a pivotal role in our confidence.

Our brain is a marvel, and when it comes to confidence, specific areas light up and get into action. One of the primary regions is the prefrontal cortex. This area is associated with decision-making, social interactions, and personality expression. When we're feeling confident, our prefrontal cortex is buzzing with activity.

Another key player is the striatum, a part of our brain involved in reward and pleasure. Think of those moments when you've achieved something, and that rush of happiness floods in; that's the striatum celebrating with you!

According to Dr. Stacie Grossman Bloom, as discussed in a Forbes article, when we feel confident, we activate what's known as "" of the brain, which includes regions like the striatum and prefrontal cortex. This activation makes us literally feel good, and it's contagious, influencing those around us.

But remember, our brain is complex, and many factors can influence these regions. Emotions, past experiences, and even our environment can play a role. However, understanding the primary players in the confidence game gives us a clearer picture of the science behind our self-belief. So, let's continue our journey, diving deeper into the wonders of our brain and its role in shaping our confidence!

The Role of Neurotransmitters

Neurotransmitters are like the brain's chemical messengers. They transmit signals between nerve cells, influencing everything from mood to muscle movement. When it comes to confidence and self-esteem, certain neurotransmitters play a starring role.

Serotonin, for instance, is a big player in this arena. According to an article from ASCD titled, fluctuations in serotonin levels can significantly impact our self-esteem. High serotonin levels in the brain are associated with feelings of calm, smooth motor coordination, and a boost in self-esteem. On the flip side, low serotonin levels can lead to irritability, impulsiveness, and even aggressive behaviors.

But serotonin isn't the only neurotransmitter in the spotlight. Dopamine, often dubbed the "feel-good" neurotransmitter, is linked to pleasure, reward, and motivation. When we achieve a goal or receive positive feedback, dopamine levels surge, giving us that euphoric feeling of accomplishment.

However, it's essential to remember that our brain's chemistry is a delicate balance. External factors, like stress, trauma, or even our diet, can influence neurotransmitter levels. For instance, certain foods can enhance serotonin production, while chronic stress might deplete it.

In the grand scheme of things, understanding the role of neurotransmitters in confidence provides us with valuable insights. It's a reminder that our feelings of self-worth and self-belief aren't just abstract concepts; they're deeply rooted in our biology. So, as we continue our journey, let's keep in mind that every thought, emotion, and reaction is a beautiful dance of chemicals in our brain. And with the right knowledge, we can tune into this dance and sway to the rhythm of confidence!

Neuroplasticity and Change

Let's dive into one of the most groundbreaking discoveries in neuroscience: neuroplasticity. It's a fancy term, but in essence, it's all about our brain's incredible ability to change and adapt.

Historically, scientists believed that our brains stopped growing after childhood. But, as highlighted in , modern research has debunked this myth. Our brains can continue to grow, change, and adapt throughout our lives. This means that the neural pathways and connections in our brains aren't set in stone. They can be reshaped, molded, and altered based on our experiences.

Now, why is this so exciting when we talk about confidence? Because it means that no matter our past experiences or current self-beliefs, our brains have the capacity to rewire and adapt. If we've been stuck in patterns of self-doubt or negative thinking, neuroplasticity offers hope. With the right tools, techniques, and mindset, we can literally rewire our brains to foster more confidence and positive self-belief.

Imagine your brain as a garden. Even if some parts have been neglected or overrun with weeds (negative thoughts), with care, attention, and the right tools, you can cultivate a lush, thriving garden of self-confidence and self-worth.

So, as we delve deeper into the world of confidence, remember this: your brain is on your side. It's adaptable, malleable, and ready to support you on your journey to a more confident you. Let's harness the power of neuroplasticity and pave our path to unwavering self-belief!

Sub-chapter 2.2: How Positive Affirmations Work

Rewiring the Brain

The human brain is a dynamic entity, constantly evolving and adapting. One of the most profound ways we can influence our brain's wiring is through positive affirmations. But how does this work?

Every moment of every day, our body undergoes physical changes in response to our thoughts. Just by thinking about something, our brain sends signals and releases neuro-transmitters, which control almost all of our body's functions, including our mood and feelings. Over time, with repetition, it's been scientifically proven that our thoughts can change our brain, our cells, and even our genes, as highlighted in .

Positive affirmations are intentional thoughts we create to support, encourage, and calm our brain and body. They can challenge negative or anxiety-producing thoughts and beliefs or simply offer general supportive thoughts. When we use affirmations, we activate the brain's reward centers, specifically the ventral striatum and ventromedial prefrontal cortex. These areas respond similarly to other pleasurable experiences, like enjoying a favorite meal or achieving a goal.

Moreover, a study using functional magnetic resonance imaging (fMRI) showed that affirmations activate areas of the brain connected to self-related processing. This can act as an emotional buffer against painful or threatening information. Interestingly, the study also revealed that future-oriented affirmations, like envisioning future success, created more self-affirming brain activity than recalling past achievements.

In essence, positive affirmations are like exercises for our mind. Just as we engage in physical exercises to improve our physical health, affirmations are mental repetitions that can reprogram our thinking patterns. Over time, with consistent practice, we can begin to think and act differently, harnessing the power of our brain's neuroplasticity to foster a more positive and confident self-image.

The Science of Habit Formation

The science behind habit formation is both fascinating and deeply rooted in our neurology. Habits, whether beneficial or detrimental, are routines or rituals that have become almost automatic or second nature to us. They stem from our brain's constant quest for actions that release dopamine, the reward chemical. This drive for pleasure has its origins in our evolutionary history, where seeking pleasure and avoiding discomfort were crucial for survival.

Habits are formed through a process that involves a cue, an action, and a reward. This cycle, known as the habit loop, was identified by psychologists at the Massachusetts Institute of Technology (MIT) and later popularized by journalist Charles Duhigg in his book "The Power of Habit." The loop starts with a cue, which triggers a craving for a particular outcome. This leads to a response, where we engage in behaviors to achieve that outcome. Once the outcome is achieved, a reward is felt, reinforcing the cue for the next time.

For instance, when we feel stressed (the cue), we might eat comfort food (the response) and feel momentarily better (the reward). Over time, this pattern solidifies, making it challenging to break. However, the brain's plasticity allows us to rewire these patterns. One method is self-directed neuroplasticity, where we intentionally rewire our brain to form positive habits. This method involves active reflection and was popularized by Dr. Rick Hanson, a psychologist at UC Berkeley.

In today's world, the constant search for feel-good experiences can sometimes lead us astray. While our ancestors sought comfort and calories for survival, we might seek them in unhealthy foods or unproductive behaviors. But understanding the science behind habits can empower us to make better choices. By recognizing the cues and rewards that drive our actions, we can intentionally create new, healthier habits or modify existing ones.

One effective strategy is to connect good habits with immediate rewards. For example, only listening to a favorite podcast while exercising can make the activity more appealing. Another approach is mindfulness, where reflecting on how certain behaviors make us feel can help us make better choices in the future. By understanding the science of habits, we can harness our brain's power to create lasting positive change in our lives.

Daily Rituals to Embed Positivity

Ever had one of those mornings where you hit the snooze button one too many times, and the rest of the day just feels like a chaotic mess? We've all been there. But what if I told you that starting your day with intention could change everything? Yep, it's all about those morning rituals.

Mornings set the tone for the rest of the day. If you kick things off with a positive attitude, you're more likely to have a fantastic day. But if you start with negativity, well, you get the drift. So, how can you ensure your mornings are always on the right track? By adopting a mindful morning routine!

Here are some rituals that can help you start your day with a burst of positivity:

1. Wake Up to a Tidy Home: A clutter-free environment can lead to a clutter-free mind. So, make it a habit to tidy up before hitting the sack. Waking up to a clean space can give you a fresh start and a clearer mind.

2. Prepare Ahead: Lay out your outfit and prep your meals the night before. It saves time and reduces morning stress.

3. Embrace Fresh Air: Even if it's chilly, open your windows for a bit. The fresh air can be invigorating and help you feel more connected to the world outside.

4. Digital Detox: Resist the urge to check your phone or emails first thing in the morning. Instead, focus on replenishing your energy and setting a positive tone for the day.

5. Stay Hydrated: Start your day with a glass of water. It's a simple act that can make you feel refreshed and ready to tackle the day.

6. Do What Makes You Happy: Whether it's playing with your pet, sipping tea, or listening to music, indulge in activities that bring you joy.

7. Practice Gratitude: Take a moment to reflect on the things you're thankful for. It can shift your perspective and make you appreciate the little things in life.

8. Set Intentions: Decide how you want your day to unfold. Setting intentions can give your day purpose and direction.

9. Affirmations: Positive affirmations can boost your confidence and set a positive tone for the day. Recite them out loud and let them guide your actions.

10. Plan Something Exciting: Having something to look forward to can keep you motivated throughout the day.

11. Journaling: Take a few minutes to jot down your thoughts, feelings, and goals. It's a great way to gain clarity and focus.

12. Make Your Bed: It's a small task, but it can give you a sense of accomplishment and order.

13. Skincare Routine: Taking care of your skin can make you feel pampered and boost your confidence.

14. Eat a Healthy Breakfast: Fuel your body with a nutritious meal to kickstart your day.

15. Move Your Body: Whether it's a workout, yoga, or just stretching, physical activity can energize you and set a positive tone for the day.

Remember, it's not about following all these rituals religiously. It's about finding what works for you and making it a part of your daily routine. Over time, these small acts can lead to big changes in your mindset and overall well-being.

Sub-chapter 2.3: Feedback Loops of Self-Esteem

The Cycle of Thoughts, Feelings, and Actions

Life is a dance of interconnected cycles, and when it comes to our self-esteem, the dance involves our thoughts, feelings, and actions. Let's break it down:

1. Thoughts: These are the internal dialogues, the narratives we tell ourselves. For instance, after a presentation, you might think, "I did well" or "I messed up." These thoughts are influenced by past experiences, beliefs, and external feedback. Anxious thoughts, in particular, can be persistent and intrusive, often spiraling into worst-case scenarios.

2. Feelings: Thoughts trigger emotions. If you believe you did well in the presentation, you might feel proud or relieved. On the other hand, if you think you messed up, feelings of disappointment or anxiety might arise. Emotions are complex and can be fleeting or long-lasting, depending on various factors, including our thoughts.

3. Actions: Our feelings then influence our behaviors. If you're feeling proud, you might share your success with colleagues or treat yourself. If you're anxious, you might avoid feedback or ruminate on perceived mistakes. Our actions can either reinforce our initial thoughts or challenge them.

This cycle is self-perpetuating. Our actions lead to new experiences, which give rise to fresh thoughts, sparking new emotions, and resulting in subsequent actions. Over time, these cycles can solidify, becoming automatic responses or habits. For instance, if you consistently receive positive feedback after sharing your work, you might develop a habit of seeking feedback, reinforcing a positive self-image.

However, it's essential to recognize that while we might not have direct control over every thought or emotion, we do have control over our actions. By intentionally choosing actions that challenge negative thoughts or feelings, we can start to shift the cycle in a more positive direction. For example, even if you feel anxious about a presentation, choosing to focus on the parts that went well can shift your thoughts and feelings over time.

Understanding this interconnected cycle is crucial. It empowers us to recognize where we might be getting stuck and offers insights into how we can initiate positive change.

By being mindful of this cycle and actively choosing our actions, we can influence our thoughts and feelings, fostering a more positive and robust sense of self-esteem.

Breaking Negative Feedback Loops

We've all been there - trapped in a whirlwind of negative thoughts that seem to feed off each other, spiraling into a seemingly endless loop. This is what's known as a negative feedback loop. But here's the good news: it's possible to break free from this cycle.

Imagine your mind as a busy highway. Negative thoughts are like cars speeding by, one after the other, creating a traffic jam of anxiety, doubt, and fear. But what if you could redirect this traffic, creating a smoother flow of positive, affirming thoughts?

One effective way to interrupt this cycle is by grounding yourself in the present moment. When you find yourself caught in a storm of negative thoughts, pause and ask yourself: "How am I feeling?" Then, pinpoint where in your body you feel these emotions. This simple act of self-awareness can serve as a brake, slowing down the rush of negative thoughts and allowing you to regain control.

Another strategy is to actively challenge these thoughts. Instead of passively accepting them, question their validity. Ask yourself: "Is this thought based on fact or assumption?" Often, you'll find that these thoughts are based on unfounded fears or past experiences that no longer hold relevance.

Additionally, celebrate small victories. Even if it's just a momentary feeling of relief or happiness, acknowledge it. These fleeting moments of positivity can serve as building blocks, gradually replacing the negative feedback loop with a positive one.

Lastly, practice mindfulness. By anchoring yourself in the present and observing your thoughts without judgment, you can create a mental buffer, preventing negative thoughts from gaining momentum.

Remember, breaking negative feedback loops is a journey, not a destination. It requires consistent effort and self-awareness. But with time and practice, you can shift your mindset from one dominated by negativity to one filled with positivity and hope.

Forming Positive Reinforcement Patterns

We often hear about the power of positive reinforcement, but how exactly can we harness it to foster a healthier self-esteem? Let's delve into the art of self-reinforcement.

Positive reinforcement is the act of rewarding a behavior, making it more likely to occur again in the future. When it comes to self-esteem, the behavior we're looking to reinforce is our positive self-perception and the actions that align with it.

One of the most empowering things you can do for yourself is to become your own cheerleader. Instead of relying on external validation, learn to recognize and celebrate your achievements, no matter how small. Here's how:

1. Self-Awareness: Begin by acknowledging your accomplishments. Recognize the hard work you've put in and give yourself credit for it. This shift from seeking external validation to self-praising can be transformative.

2. Tangible Rewards: Reward yourself for a job well done. It could be as simple as treating yourself to your favorite dessert or as grand as a vacation. The key is to choose rewards that resonate with you.

3. Avoid External Validation: While it's natural to seek appreciation, relying solely on external validation can be problematic. It's inconsistent and can lead to feelings of resentment or frustration. Instead, focus on self-appreciation.

4. Consistency: Make self-reinforcement a regular practice. Whether it's daily affirmations or weekly rewards, consistency is key to forming positive reinforcement patterns.

5. Plan Ahead: If you're working towards a long-term goal, break it down into smaller milestones and reward yourself at each step. This not only keeps you motivated but also reinforces positive behavior.

6. Be Patient: Forming new habits takes time. Research by Phillipa Lally suggests that it can take anywhere from two to eight months to form a new behavior pattern. So, be patient with yourself and celebrate the journey.

By actively practicing self-reinforcement, you're not just boosting your self-esteem; you're also creating a positive feedback loop that encourages more of the behaviors and mindsets that contribute to a healthy self-image.

Sub-chapter 2.4: Genetics vs. Environment

Nature vs. Nurture in Confidence Building

The age-old debate of nature versus nurture has been at the forefront of many scientific discussions, especially when it comes to traits like self-confidence. So, where does confidence truly stem from? Is it etched in our DNA, or is it sculpted by our environment?

While there's no denying that our genes play a role in our predispositions, it's a misconception to believe that self-confidence is solely a result of genetics. Yes, our parents might pass down certain traits that make us more optimistic or pessimistic. However, leading-edge neuroscientists emphasize that our biology isn't our destiny. We have a plethora of options that can positively enhance our innate sense of self-confidence. Activities like regular exercise, meditation, healthy eating, positive thinking, and consistent sleep patterns can all bolster our self-assurance.

Moreover, self-confidence is a skill, not a fixed trait. It's something that can be nurtured and developed over time. There are stages and types of self-confidence, and with the right tools and mindset, anyone can enhance their confidence levels, regardless of their genetic makeup. For instance, while some might inherit a certain level of confidence from their parents, personal experiences and choices can push them beyond that inherited level.

In essence, while our genes might set the stage, it's our experiences, choices, and environment that truly shape our confidence. It's a harmonious dance between nature and nurture, with both playing pivotal roles in the grand ballet of self-assurance.

Leveraging Both for Self-Improvement

The interplay between genetics (nature) and environment (nurture) is intricate, with both factors contributing to who we are. But instead of viewing them as opposing forces, consider them as two sides of the same coin. When leveraged together, they can be a powerful catalyst for self-improvement.

1. Recognize Your Genetic Strengths: Everyone has innate abilities or tendencies. Maybe you're naturally good at public speaking, or perhaps you have an inherent knack for problem-solving. Recognize these genetic gifts and harness them. They're your foundation.

2. Challenge Your Genetic Limitations: Just because you're predisposed to something doesn't mean you're bound by it. If you've always felt you're not a 'math person' due to family history, challenge that notion. With the right mindset and effort, you can overcome many genetic predispositions.

3. Create a Nurturing Environment: Your environment plays a pivotal role in self-improvement. Surround yourself with positive influences, be it supportive friends, educational resources, or enriching experiences. They can help nurture traits and skills that might not come naturally to you.

4. Continuous Learning: Regardless of your genetic makeup, the brain has an incredible capacity to learn and adapt. Embrace lifelong learning. Attend workshops, read books, or take up new hobbies. This not only enhances your skills but also provides environmental stimuli that can counteract or complement genetic predispositions.

5. Reflect and Adjust: Regularly assess your progress. What's working? What isn't? By understanding how nature and nurture are affecting your journey, you can make informed decisions about the next steps.

In essence, while you can't change your genes, you have control over your actions and environment. By understanding and leveraging both nature and nurture, you can pave a path of continuous self-improvement, turning potential weaknesses into strengths and maximizing your inherent talents.

Empowering Stories of Environmental Triumphs

Throughout history, countless individuals have faced seemingly insurmountable challenges, only to rise above them, proving that environment and personal determination can indeed shape destiny. Here are a few empowering tales:

1. Oprah Winfrey: Born into poverty and faced with numerous challenges in her early life, including abuse and discrimination, Oprah's environment could have easily defined her future. However, her relentless drive and determination led her

to become one of the most influential figures in media. Her story is a testament to the power of resilience and the belief that one's environment doesn't have to dictate their future.

2. Stephen Hawking: Diagnosed with ALS at 21 and given just a few years to live, Hawking's physical environment was undoubtedly challenging. However, his indomitable spirit and passion for science led him to make groundbreaking contributions to theoretical physics. His life story showcases that physical limitations can be transcended by a powerful mind.

3. Malala Yousafzai: Growing up in a region where girls were often denied education, Malala became an advocate for girls' rights to learn. Despite facing life-threatening adversity, she continued her advocacy, proving that one's environment can be both a challenge and a catalyst for change.

These stories remind us that while genetics and environment play roles in shaping us, our choices, determination, and resilience can lead us to paths of greatness. It's not just about the cards we're dealt, but how we choose to play them.

Sub-chapter 2.5: Hormonal Influences

The Role of Testosterone and Estrogen

Hormones play a significant role in influencing our behavior, mood, and even our self-confidence. Among these, testosterone and estrogen stand out for their profound impact on our psyche.

Testosterone: Often dubbed the 'confidence hormone,' testosterone is associated with assertiveness, competitiveness, and risk-taking. Both men and women produce testosterone, but it's typically higher in men. Elevated levels of this hormone have been linked to increased feelings of self-worth and confidence. For instance, individuals with higher testosterone levels are often more willing to take risks and face challenges head-on. It's not just about physical prowess; this hormone also influences mental resilience and determination.

Estrogen: Predominantly a female hormone, estrogen plays a crucial role in mood regulation. It's been observed that fluctuating estrogen levels, such as during menstrual cycles, can impact a woman's self-perception and confidence. While estrogen is essential for various bodily functions, its influence on mood and behavior is undeniable. A balanced level of estrogen often leads to feelings of well-being and positivity.

However, it's essential to note that hormones are just one piece of the puzzle. While they do influence our behavior and feelings, our environment, experiences, and choices play equally vital roles in shaping our self-confidence. It's the interplay of biology and experience that crafts our unique journey of self-discovery and growth.

Stress Hormones and Their Impact

The stress hormone, cortisol, plays a significant role in our mental and physical well-being. Elevated cortisol levels, often a result of chronic stress, can interfere with learning, memory, immune function, and even bone density. It can lead to weight gain, increased blood pressure, cholesterol, heart disease, and a higher risk for depression and mental illnesses. Especially during adolescence, elevated cortisol levels can trigger mental health issues and reduce resilience.

Cortisol is released as a response to fear or stress, part of the fight-or-flight mechanism. This mechanism was defined by biochemist Hans Selye in 1936, distinguishing between eustress (good stress) and distress (bad stress). While eustress can be invigorating and goal-oriented, distress, without a proper outlet, can lead to built-up cortisol levels, negatively impacting the mind and body.

Physical activity, mindfulness, social connectivity, laughter, and music are some of the ways to reduce cortisol levels. For instance, regular physical activity can decrease fear, boost self-confidence, resilience, and fortitude, ultimately reducing cortisol. Mindfulness and meditation practices, even if for a few minutes daily, can significantly reduce stress and anxiety. Social connections, whether with family, friends, or even online, can foster feelings of connectivity, reducing cortisol. Laughter, humor, and music also play a crucial role in mood elevation and cortisol reduction.

In today's digital age, where stressors are abundant, understanding the impact of cortisol and finding ways to manage and reduce its levels is crucial for mental and physical health. By making simple lifestyle choices, one can effectively manage stress and lead a healthier, more balanced life.

Balancing Body Chemistry Through Lifestyle

Our body's chemistry, particularly our hormonal balance, plays a pivotal role in our overall well-being. While certain factors might be beyond our control, our lifestyle choices can significantly influence our body's hormonal equilibrium. Here's how you can steer your body towards a balanced state:

1. Nutrition: A balanced diet rich in whole foods, healthy fats, and lean proteins can stabilize hormone levels. Foods like avocados, fatty fish, and quinoa are not only nutritious but also help in regulating hormones.

2. Physical Activity: Regular exercise can boost endorphin levels, often termed 'feel-good hormones.' Whether it's a brisk walk, yoga, or high-intensity interval training, find what resonates with you and stick to it.

3. Sleep: Never underestimate the power of a good night's sleep. Adequate rest ensures the body can produce and regulate essential hormones effectively.

4. Stress Management: Chronic stress can wreak havoc on your hormones. Incorporate relaxation techniques such as meditation, deep breathing exercises, or even journaling to keep stress at bay.

5. Limit Stimulants: Overconsumption of caffeine and alcohol can disrupt hormonal balance. Moderation is key.

6. Stay Hydrated: Drinking enough water supports cellular functions, including hormone production and regulation.

7. Limit Sugar and Processed Foods: High sugar intake can lead to imbalances in insulin, cortisol, and other hormones. Opt for natural sweeteners and whole foods.

By making conscious lifestyle choices, you can create an environment where your body thrives. Remember, it's not about drastic changes but consistent, small steps that lead to a harmonious body chemistry. Balancing hormones is not just about feeling good; it's about optimizing your body's potential and leading a fulfilling, healthy life.

Chapter Four

Daily Habits to Foster Confidence

"We first make our habits, then our habits make us." – John Dryden

Introduction

Reflecting on Dryden's profound words, it becomes evident that the rituals we embed in our daily lives shape our very essence. The foundation of our day, from the moment we open our eyes to the world to the instant we drift into dreams, dictates the elevation of our life. It's not just about the monumental decisions or life-altering events; it's the small, consistent habits that carve our path towards unwavering confidence.

As you journey through this chapter, consider it a warm invitation to introspect. Dive deep into your daily routines, the choices you make, the thoughts you entertain, and the actions you repeat. Recognize their power. Understand that by intentionally cultivating confidence-boosting habits, you're not just enhancing a day; you're elevating a lifetime.

So, dear reader, let's embark on this exploration together. Let's discover the daily habits that not only foster confidence but also transform it into a second nature, ensuring that every step you take is one of assurance, poise, and undeniable strength.

Sub-chapter 3.1: Morning Rituals for a Confident Start

The Science of How Our Morning Sets the Tone for the Day

The way we begin our day has a profound impact on our mood, productivity, and overall well-being. Scientifically speaking, our morning routines can either set us up for success or lead us down a path of stress and inefficiency.

During the early hours, our brain is in a state called the "alpha phase," a period of heightened creativity and reduced mental resistance. This makes it the optimal time for activities like meditation, visualization, and setting intentions. By tapping into this state, we can harness its power to shape our mindset for the day ahead.

Moreover, cortisol, our body's primary stress hormone, has its peak secretion in the first 30 minutes after waking. A calm and structured morning can help regulate its release, ensuring we don't start our day in a state of heightened stress.

Consistency in our morning routine also plays a pivotal role. Our brain thrives on predictability. By establishing a set pattern of activities each morning, we train our brain to anticipate and prepare for the day, leading to increased focus and clarity.

In essence, the science is clear: a purposeful morning routine not only sets the tone for our day but also lays the foundation for a confident, productive, and fulfilling life.

Personal Anecdotes on the Transformation Brought by Intentional Mornings

A few years ago, I stumbled upon an article by Hal Elrod about the 'Miracle Morning.' Intrigued, I decided to give it a shot. The transformation was nothing short of miraculous. Before this, my mornings were a blur of snoozed alarms, rushed breakfasts, and frantic scrambles. But with an intentional morning routine, everything shifted.

I began by dedicating the first ten minutes after waking to gratitude journaling. This simple act changed my perspective, making me more appreciative of life's blessings. Next, I incorporated a 20-minute meditation session. The calmness it brought was palpable, allowing me to face challenges with a serene mind.

But the most significant change was the incorporation of a morning workout. A friend once told me, "Sweat in the morning, before your brain figures out what you're doing!" And she was right. Those early morning endorphins became my daily dose of natural confidence.

I also came across a quote by Laura Vanderkam, author of "What the Most Successful People Do Before Breakfast," where she mentioned, "Mornings are the realm of the proactive." It resonated deeply, reinforcing my belief in the power of intentional mornings.

By reshaping my mornings, I didn't just change a part of my day; I transformed my entire life.

Tips for Creating a Personalized Morning Routine

Crafting a morning routine that aligns with your individual goals and lifestyle is essential for starting each day on the right foot. Here are some tips to help you create a routine that resonates with you:

1. Self-Reflection: Begin by understanding what you want to achieve. Is it mental clarity, physical fitness, or perhaps spiritual growth? Your goals will shape your routine.

2. Start Small: Don't overhaul your entire morning immediately. Introduce one new habit at a time. As it becomes a part of your routine, add another.

3. Prioritize Hydration: Start your day with a glass of water. It's a simple act that kickstarts your metabolism and hydrates your body.

4. Mindful Moments: Whether it's meditation, journaling, or simply sitting in silence, dedicate a few minutes to mindfulness. It sets a calm and focused tone for the day.

5. Move Your Body: Physical activity, be it stretching, yoga, or a full-blown work-out, releases endorphins that boost mood and energy.

6. Plan Ahead: Before diving into the day, take a moment to review your tasks. Knowing your priorities can make your day more productive and less chaotic.

7. Personal Touch: Your morning routine should resonate with you. If you love music, maybe start with a morning playlist. If reading inspires you, dedicate a few minutes to a book.

Remember, the best morning routine is the one that's tailored to you. It's not about mimicking someone else's habits but about finding what genuinely uplifts and prepares you for the day ahead. As Robin Sharma once said, "Your days are your life in miniature. As you live your days, so you craft your life."

Sub-chapter 3.2: The Power of Positive Self-talk

The Impact of Our Internal Dialogue on Our Confidence

Our internal dialogue, the constant stream of thoughts and self-talk that runs through our minds, plays a pivotal role in shaping our confidence. It's like the background music to our lives, subtly influencing our emotions, actions, and overall self-perception.

When this dialogue is positive, it acts as a powerful ally. It reinforces our self-worth, reminds us of our capabilities, and propels us forward even in the face of challenges. Think of it as your personal cheerleader, always rooting for you, reminding you of past victories, and encouraging you to take that next step.

Conversely, negative self-talk can be our greatest adversary. It magnifies our flaws, dwells on past mistakes, and paints a bleak picture of the future. Over time, this erodes our self-confidence, making us second-guess our decisions and shy away from opportunities.

Dr. Ethan Kross from the University of Michigan conducted studies on the topic and found that the way we talk to ourselves, especially the pronouns we use, can distance us from our emotions, allowing for more rational decision-making. By referring to oneself in the third person, individuals can create an emotional distance and view situations more objectively.

In essence, by being mindful of our internal dialogue and intentionally steering it towards positivity, we can harness its power to bolster our confidence and navigate life with greater assurance.

Strategies to Catch, Challenge, and Change Negative Self-

talk

Patterns

Negative self-talk can be a sneaky saboteur, often slipping into our thoughts without us even noticing. But with intention and practice, we can rewire these patterns. Here are some strategies to help you catch, challenge, and change negative self-talk:

1. Awareness is Key: The first step is recognizing when you're indulging in negative self-talk. Pay attention to moments when you feel down or demotivated. What were you telling yourself?

2. Journaling: Writing down your thoughts can be illuminating. It provides a tangible record of your self-talk, making patterns easier to spot.

3. Question the Thought: Challenge the validity of your negative thoughts. Ask yourself, "Is this really true? Is there evidence to support this belief? Could there be another perspective?"

4. Positive Affirmations: Replace negative thoughts with positive affirmations. For instance, change "I can't do this" to "I'll do the best I can."

5. Mindfulness and Meditation: These practices help you stay present and become more attuned to your thoughts, making it easier to catch negative patterns.

6. Seek Feedback: Sometimes, we're our own harshest critics. Talk to trusted friends or family. They can offer a more objective view and help you challenge unfounded negative beliefs.

7. Professional Help: If negative self-talk is deeply ingrained or leading to feelings

of depression or anxiety, consider seeking therapy. A professional can provide tools and strategies tailored to your needs.

Remember, changing thought patterns is a journey. Celebrate small victories and be patient with yourself. Over time, with consistent effort, you can shift from being your own critic to your biggest cheerleader.

Incorporating Affirmations and Mantras into Daily Routines

Affirmations and mantras are powerful tools that can reshape our mindset, instill positivity, and bolster confidence. These short, impactful statements serve as reminders of our worth, capabilities, and aspirations. Here's how to seamlessly weave them into your daily routines:

1. Start the Day Right: Begin each morning by reciting a chosen affirmation. It could be as simple as "Today is a new day, and I am ready for it."

2. Mirror Talk: While getting ready, look into the mirror and repeat your mantra. This act of self-affirmation, combined with your reflection, reinforces the message.

3. Affirmation Alarms: Set periodic reminders on your phone. When they go off, take a moment to pause and recite your affirmation.

4. Journaling: Dedicate a few minutes each day to write down affirmations in a journal. The act of writing reinforces the message and serves as a visual reminder.

5. Nightly Reflection: Before bed, reflect on your day and recite a mantra that resonates with your feelings or aspirations for the next day.

6. Sticky Notes: Place affirmation notes in strategic locations – your bathroom mirror, computer screen, or fridge. These visual cues serve as constant reminders.

7. Community Support: Share your affirmations with friends or family. Saying them out loud to someone else can amplify their impact.

Remember, the key to effective affirmations is consistency and belief. Choose words that resonate with you, and recite them with conviction. Over time, these positive statements will become ingrained in your psyche, transforming your mindset and elevating your confidence.

Sub-chapter 3.3: Dressing for Success

How Our Attire Influences Our Mindset and the Perceptions of Others

The clothes we wear do more than just cover our bodies; they have a profound impact on our mindset and how others perceive us. Let's delve into this fascinating interplay between attire and psychology.

1. Boosting Self-Confidence: Ever noticed how wearing your favorite outfit can instantly lift your spirits? There's a psychological reason behind it. Dressing well boosts our self-confidence, making us feel more capable and ready to tackle challenges.

2. Enclothed Cognition: This term refers to the systematic influence that clothes have on the wearer's psychological processes. For instance, wearing formal attire can make individuals feel more authoritative, trustworthy, and competent.

3. First Impressions Matter: Within seconds of meeting someone, we form an opinion about them based on their attire. Dressing appropriately for an occasion signals respect, professionalism, and attention to detail.

4. Mood Regulation: Clothes can also serve as mood regulators. Bright colors might uplift our spirits, while cozy fabrics can provide comfort on a gloomy day.

5. Social Identity: Our attire often reflects our social identity and group affiliations. It can be a powerful tool to convey our personal brand and values.

6. Performance Enhancement: Studies have shown that students wearing formal clothes perform better in negotiations and abstract thinking tasks compared to those in casual wear.

In essence, our attire acts as a non-verbal communication tool, influencing not only how others perceive us but also how we perceive ourselves. As Mark Twain aptly put it, "Clothes make the man. Naked people have little or no influence on society." So, the next time you're selecting an outfit, remember the power it holds in shaping your day and interactions.

Tips for Cultivating a Personal Style that Exudes Confidence Without Compromising Comfort

Dressing with confidence doesn't mean you have to sacrifice comfort. In fact, when you feel good in what you're wearing, your confidence naturally shines through. Here are some tips to help you strike that perfect balance:

1. Know Your Body: Understanding your body type and what silhouettes flatter you most can be a game-changer. When you wear clothes that fit well and accentuate your best features, you'll feel both comfortable and confident.

2. Invest in Staples: Quality over quantity always wins. Invest in a few timeless pieces that can be mixed and matched for various occasions. Think of a well-fitted blazer, a pair of comfortable heels, or a versatile white shirt.

3. Prioritize Comfort: Always consider the fabric and fit. Breathable materials like cotton or linen and stretchable fabrics can offer both style and ease.

4. Accessorize Wisely: Accessories can elevate a simple outfit. However, ensure they don't become a source of discomfort. For instance, if heavy earrings bother you, opt for studs or lightweight hoops.

5. Personal Touch: Your style should reflect your personality Whether it's a signature color, pattern, or accessory, let it be a representation of you.

6. Footwear Matters: A stylish yet comfortable pair of shoes can make or break your day. Consider cushioned insoles, arch support, and roomy toe boxes when choosing footwear.

7. Trial Runs: Before an important event, do a trial run with your outfit. Walk around, sit, and move to ensure you're at ease.

Remember, confidence comes from feeling good inside and out. Your attire should be an extension of your inner self, radiating the confidence you feel within, all while ensuring you're at ease.

The Psychological Boost of "Power Outfits" and Their Role in Crucial Scenarios

The concept of "power outfits" isn't just a fashion fad; it's deeply rooted in psychology. These are the outfits that make you stand taller, speak more confidently, and feel invincible. Let's delve into the transformative power of these garments:

1. Instant Confidence Boost: Just as a superhero feels empowered by their cape, a well-chosen outfit can provide an immediate surge of self-assuredness. It's not about the clothes per se, but the feelings they evoke.

2. Setting the Tone: In high-stakes scenarios, like job interviews or important meetings, power outfits act as armor. They set the tone, signaling professionalism and competence before you even utter a word.

3. Memory Anchors: Often, we associate certain outfits with past successes. Wearing them can evoke those triumphant feelings, serving as a reminder of our capabilities.

4. Non-verbal Communication: Clothes communicate. A power outfit sends a clear message about your intentions, aspirations, and self-worth.

5. Mental Shift: Dressing the part can lead to a mental shift, making you more aligned with the role you're playing. For instance, wearing formal attire might make you feel more authoritative and focused.

6. Empowerment in Vulnerable Situations: In situations where you might feel vulnerable or out of place, a power outfit acts as a shield, boosting your morale and resilience.

In essence, power outfits are more than just clothes. They're tools of empowerment, helping you navigate crucial scenarios with grace and confidence. So, the next time you face a challenging situation, remember the strength that lies in your wardrobe. Choose wisely, and let your attire amplify your inner strength.

Sub-chapter 3.4: Nurturing the Mind-Body Connection

The Ripple Effect of Physical Well-being on Mental Confidence

The intricate dance between our physical well-being and mental confidence is a testament to the profound mind-body connection. When we nurture one, the other naturally flourishes. Let's explore this symbiotic relationship:

1. Endorphin Release: Physical activities, especially exercise, release endorphins—our body's natural feel-good chemicals. These not only alleviate pain but also boost our mood, leading to heightened confidence.

2. Improved Self-image: Taking care of our physical health, be it through regular exercise, a balanced diet, or adequate sleep, often results in a better self-image. When we feel good about our bodies, our mental confidence soars.

3. Stress Reduction: Physical well-being directly impacts our stress levels. Activities like yoga, meditation, or even a simple walk can act as potent stress-busters, paving the way for a more confident mindset.

4. Enhanced Cognitive Function: A healthy body supports a healthy brain. Physical well-being can lead to improved memory, sharper focus, and better decision-making—all vital components of confidence.

5. Resilience Building: Overcoming physical challenges, whether it's mastering a new sport or recovering from an illness, builds resilience. This mental toughness translates into confidence in other areas of life.

6. Holistic Health: Physical health doesn't operate in isolation. It's intertwined with our emotional, social, and mental well-being. When we prioritize our physical health, we're also nurturing our overall well-being, which naturally boosts confidence.

In essence, the journey to mental confidence often begins with the steps we take to ensure our physical well-being. By recognizing and harnessing this connection, we set ourselves up for a life brimming with confidence and vitality.

Simple Daily Exercises and Activities that Enhance Posture, Poise, and Presence

Our posture, poise, and presence play a pivotal role in how we feel and how we're perceived by others. By incorporating simple daily exercises and activities, we can significantly enhance these aspects, leading to a more confident and commanding presence. Here's how:

1. Wall Angels: Stand with your back against a wall, arms extended out. Slowly raise them above your head and back down, mimicking the motion of a snow angel. This strengthens the back and shoulder muscles, promoting better posture.

2. Plank: A core-strengthening exercise, the plank not only enhances posture but also builds endurance. Start with short intervals and gradually increase the duration.

3. Mindful Walking: Instead of rushing from one place to another, practice mindful walking. Feel each step, stand tall, and maintain a steady breathing rhythm. This simple act can greatly improve posture and presence.

4. Stretching: Incorporate daily stretches, especially targeting the neck, shoulders, and back. This releases tension and helps in maintaining an upright posture.

5. Mirror Practice: Spend a few minutes each day practicing poise in front of a mirror. Focus on standing tall, maintaining eye contact, and practicing confident gestures.

6. Breathing Exercises: Deep breathing not only calms the mind but also helps in maintaining a poised stance. Practice diaphragmatic breathing to enhance both poise and presence.

7. Dance: Whether it's a structured form like ballet or just freestyle dancing to your favorite tunes, dancing helps improve posture, balance, and body awareness.

Remember, the key is consistency. By incorporating these simple exercises and activities into your daily routine, you'll not only enhance your physical posture but also exude a confidence that's palpable.

The Role of Nutrition in Fueling Confidence from the Inside Out

What we consume doesn't just affect our physical health; it has a profound impact on our mental well-being and, by extension, our confidence. Let's delve into the transformative power of nutrition:

1. Brain Boosters: Omega-3 fatty acids, found in fish like salmon and walnuts, have been linked to improved cognitive function and mood regulation. A sharper mind often translates to heightened confidence.

2. Mood Modulators: Foods rich in tryptophan, like turkey and bananas, aid in the production of serotonin, the "feel-good" neurotransmitter. A balanced mood can be a solid foundation for confidence.

3. Gut-Brain Connection: Probiotics found in yogurt and fermented foods support gut health, which is intricately linked to mental well-being. A healthy gut can lead to a more positive and confident mindset.

4. Energy Enhancers: Complex carbohydrates, like whole grains and legumes, provide sustained energy, preventing the mood and energy dips that can dent confidence.

5. Mineral Magic: Magnesium, found in leafy greens and nuts, plays a role in over 300 enzymatic reactions in the body, including those that regulate mood.

6. Stay Hydrated: Even mild dehydration can affect mood and cognitive function. Drinking adequate water supports overall well-being and confidence.

7. Limit Sugar: Excessive sugar intake can lead to energy crashes and mood swings, undermining confidence. Opt for natural sweeteners and whole fruits instead.

In essence, by making intentional food choices, we can fuel our confidence from the inside out. It's not just about looking good but feeling good at the core, and the right nutrition plays a pivotal role in that journey.

Sub-chapter 3.5: Nightly Reflection and Visualization

The Importance of Ending the Day on a Note of Gratitude and Forward Vision

As the day winds down, our minds often replay the events, conversations, and emotions we've experienced. This reflection can either uplift us or weigh us down. That's where the power of gratitude and forward vision comes into play.

1. Gratitude Grounding: Taking a moment to acknowledge and appreciate the good in our day, no matter how small, shifts our focus from what went wrong to what went right. This simple act releases feel-good hormones, reduces stress, and fosters a positive mindset. Studies have shown that individuals who practice gratitude consistently report fewer symptoms of illness, feel better about their lives as a whole, and are more optimistic about the future.

2. Forward Vision: Visualizing positive outcomes for the next day or the near future acts as a beacon of hope. This mental rehearsal not only prepares us for challenges but also instills a sense of purpose and direction.

3. The Compound Effect: Over time, these nightly practices compound. They not only improve sleep quality but also cultivate a resilient and confident mindset, ready to tackle the challenges of a new day.

In essence, ending the day with gratitude and a forward vision is like setting a positive intention for the next. It's a gentle reminder that, despite the ups and downs, there's always something to be thankful for and a brighter tomorrow to look forward to.

Techniques for Reflective Journaling and Visualizing Future Successes

Reflective journaling and visualization are powerful tools that can transform our mindset, helping us process emotions, set intentions, and visualize our goals. Here's how to harness their potential:

1. Start Simple with Reflective Journaling: Begin with a gratitude list. Jot down three things you're thankful for from the day. This simple act can shift your focus from challenges to blessings, fostering a positive mindset.

2. Prompted Entries: If you're unsure what to write, use prompts like, "What did I learn today?", "How did I overcome challenges?", or "What am I looking forward to tomorrow?". These questions can guide your reflection and help you delve deeper into your feelings.

3. Visualize in Detail: For visualization, find a quiet space, close your eyes, and vividly imagine a future success. Feel the emotions, hear the sounds, and see the colors. The more detailed your visualization, the more impactful it will be.

4. Combine Both Techniques: After journaling, take a moment to visualize a positive outcome related to what you've written. For instance, if you journaled about a challenge, visualize yourself overcoming it with grace and confidence.

5. Consistency is Key: Like any habit, the more consistently you practice reflective journaling and visualization, the more profound their impact will be on your mindset and confidence.

Incorporating these techniques into your nightly routine can be a game-changer. They not only provide clarity and closure to your day but also set a positive tone for the days to come, fueling your journey towards greater confidence and success.

Crafting a Nighttime Ritual that Ensures Restful Sleep and Rejuvenated Mornings

A restful night's sleep is the cornerstone of a confident and energetic day. Crafting a nighttime ritual is essential to ensure you wake up rejuvenated and ready to tackle the challenges ahead. Here's how to create a routine that promotes restful sleep:

1. Digital Detox: Begin by setting aside electronic devices at least an hour before

bedtime. The blue light emitted by screens can interfere with the production of melatonin, a hormone that regulates sleep.

2. Relaxation Techniques: Incorporate relaxation methods such as deep breathing exercises, progressive muscle relaxation, or meditation. These practices help calm the mind and prepare the body for sleep.

3. Aromatherapy: Consider using essential oils like lavender or chamomile, known for their sleep-inducing properties. A few drops on your pillow or in a diffuser can set a calming ambiance.

4. Reading: Instead of screens, pick up a physical book. Reading can be a great way to wind down, but opt for light, non-stimulating content.

5. Consistent Sleep Schedule: Go to bed and wake up at the same time every day, even on weekends. This consistency reinforces your body's sleep-wake cycle.

6. Comfortable Sleep Environment: Ensure your bedroom is conducive to sleep. This includes a comfortable mattress, dark curtains, and a cool room temperature.

By prioritizing sleep and crafting a ritual that suits your needs, you're setting the stage for a day filled with confidence, clarity, and energy. Remember, the quality of your sleep directly impacts your mood, productivity, and overall well-being. So, invest in your nighttime routine, and you'll reap the benefits in the morning and beyond.

Conclusion to Chapter 3: Daily Habits to Foster Confidence

Confidence, dear reader, is not a mountaintop we reach, plant a flag, and then reside upon forever. It's a winding path, a journey with its ups and downs, scenic views, and challenging terrains. Every step you take, every habit you cultivate, is a testament to your commitment to this journey.

The daily rituals and habits we've explored in this chapter aren't mere tasks to check off a list. They are acts of self-love, small yet significant choices that, over time, construct the bridge to your most confident self. Each morning ritual, each positive affirmation, each moment of reflection is a brick in the path of your self-assured future.

As you move forward, remember that every day won't be perfect. There will be days when doubt might creep in, when the world might seem overwhelming. But it's on these days that your commitment to these habits will shine the brightest, guiding you back to your path.

So, embrace this journey with an open heart. Celebrate the small victories, learn from the setbacks, and always, always remember: you're not just building confidence; you're crafting a love letter to yourself, one day at a time.

Chapter Five

Embracing Vulnerability

The Strength in Softness

"Vulnerability is not winning or losing; it's having the courage to show up and be seen when we have no control over the outcome." – Brené Brown

In a world that often equates strength with stoicism and vulnerability with weakness, it's easy to build walls around our true selves. We're conditioned to believe that showing our soft side is an invitation for hurt. But what if we've got it all wrong?

What if, within vulnerability, lies an unmatched power and authenticity? This chapter invites you on a transformative journey, one where we'll dismantle long-held myths and discover the profound strength in embracing our vulnerabilities. It's about understanding that our softness doesn't diminish our power; it amplifies it.

By allowing ourselves to be seen, to feel deeply, and to share our authentic stories, we not only connect more genuinely with others but also foster a deeper, more compassionate relationship with ourselves. Let's embark on this exploration together, shedding the weight of societal expectations and stepping into a space where vulnerability is celebrated as the ultimate form of courageous living.

Sub-chapter 4.1: The Myths of Vulnerability

Societal Misconceptions About Showing Weakness

From a young age, many of us are taught to "toughen up," to hide our tears, and to suppress our emotions. Society often paints a picture where vulnerability is synonymous with weakness. This misconception is deeply rooted in cultural narratives that equate emotional openness with a lack of resilience or strength. Think about the countless movies where the stoic hero, unyielding and unemotional, is celebrated, while those who wear their hearts on their sleeves are often portrayed as fragile or overly sensitive.

These societal standards have led many to believe that showing any sign of "softness" is an invitation for ridicule or exploitation. We're conditioned to think that if we let our guard down, we're setting ourselves up for disappointment or hurt. But this couldn't be further from the truth. In reality, vulnerability is not about weakness; it's about authenticity. It's about having the courage to show up as our true selves, even when it's uncomfortable or scary.

By buying into these misconceptions, we rob ourselves of genuine connections and authentic living. It's time to challenge these outdated beliefs and recognize that there's immense strength in allowing ourselves to be seen, flaws and all

How Vulnerability Breeds Authenticity

In a world saturated with curated images and filtered realities, authenticity stands out as a rare gem. But where does this authenticity stem from? The answer is vulnerability. Vulnerability is the birthplace of authenticity. It's the raw, unfiltered core of who we are, and when we embrace it, we present our most genuine selves to the world.

When we shield ourselves from vulnerability, we often put on masks, trying to fit into molds that society deems acceptable. This facade might protect us momentarily from potential judgments or criticisms, but it also distances us from our true essence. On the other hand, when we allow ourselves to be vulnerable, we shed these pretenses and societal expectations. We stop trying to be who we think we should be and start being who we truly are.

Embracing vulnerability means acknowledging our imperfections, our fears, our desires, and our dreams. It's about being honest with ourselves and with others. This honesty, this raw openness, is what breeds authenticity. It's a magnetic quality that draws people in, fostering deeper connections and more meaningful interactions. In a world that often values superficiality, choosing vulnerability and, by extension, authenticity, is a revolutionary act. It's a choice to live with integrity, aligning our external actions with our internal truths.

Case Studies: Successful Figures Who Embraced Vulnerability

Throughout history, many successful figures have shown that embracing vulnerability can be a powerful catalyst for growth and achievement. Let's delve into a few notable examples:

1. Brené Brown: A research professor and bestselling author, Brené's ground-breaking work on vulnerability has transformed how we view the concept. Her TED Talk on the power of vulnerability has garnered millions of views. By sharing her own struggles with shame and vulnerability, she has inspired countless others to embrace their imperfections and live authentically.

2. Steve Jobs: The co-founder of Apple, Jobs was known for his relentless pursuit of perfection. Yet, in his famous Stanford commencement speech, he opened up about his fears, failures, and the moments he felt most vulnerable. This candidness showcased a side of Jobs that many hadn't seen, highlighting the depth behind his genius.

3. J.K. Rowling: The renowned author of the "Harry Potter" series, Rowling faced numerous rejections before her work was finally published. She has spoken openly about her struggles with depression and the challenges she faced as a single mother living on welfare. By sharing her story of perseverance and vulnerability, Rowling has inspired millions to believe in the magic of resilience and determination.

These figures, among many others, demonstrate that vulnerability isn't a weakness but a strength. By embracing their vulnerabilities, they've not only achieved personal success but have also made lasting impacts in their respective fields. Their stories serve as powerful reminders that vulnerability can be the key to unlocking our fullest potential.

Sub-chapter 4.2: Vulnerability in Relationships

Fostering Deeper Connections

In the realm of relationships, vulnerability often acts as the bridge to deeper, more meaningful connections. It's a universal truth that relationships thrive on trust, understanding, and emotional intimacy. And guess what? All these elements are intertwined with vulnerability.

Imagine a scenario where two individuals are always guarded, never revealing their true feelings or fears. Such a relationship would lack depth and emotional resonance. Now, contrast this with a relationship where both partners are open about their insecurities, dreams, and even past traumas. The latter relationship is bound to be richer, filled with understanding and empathy.

Being vulnerable means letting your guard down and allowing another person to see the real you, warts and all. It's about sharing those stories, feelings, and thoughts that you might usually keep hidden. And while this might seem daunting, it's this very act that paves the way for genuine connections.

Dr. Brené Brown, a renowned researcher on vulnerability, once said, "Vulnerability is the birthplace of love, belonging, joy, courage, empathy, and creativity." By embracing vulnerability in our relationships, we not only foster deeper connections but also cultivate an environment where love and understanding flourish.

Remember, it's the imperfections, the shared struggles, and the mutual support during tough times that make relationships truly special. Embracing vulnerability is the key to unlocking these beautiful aspects of any relationship.

The Trust-Vulnerability Cycle

The trust-vulnerability cycle is a delicate dance that plays out in every relationship, from friendships to romantic partnerships. It's a cycle that can either strengthen bonds or break them, depending on how it's navigated.

Imagine trust and vulnerability as two sides of the same coin. To trust someone, you must be willing to be vulnerable with them. This means opening up, sharing your fears, hopes, and dreams, and exposing parts of yourself that you might usually keep hidden. When you do this, you're essentially handing them a piece of your heart and saying, "I trust you not to hurt this."

On the flip side, when someone shows vulnerability towards you, it's a sign that they trust you. They believe in your capacity to understand, empathize, and not exploit their openness. When you honor that trust, it deepens the bond between you.

However, the cycle can be disrupted. If trust is broken, vulnerability retreats. It's a protective mechanism. Why would anyone want to be open and exposed if they fear getting hurt? Rebuilding trust once it's broken is a challenging endeavor and requires both parties to once again embrace vulnerability.

But here's the beautiful part: every time you successfully navigate this cycle, the relationship grows stronger. The trust deepens, and the willingness to be vulnerable increases. Over time, this creates an unbreakable bond between individuals, a connection rooted in mutual respect and understanding.

In essence, the trust-vulnerability cycle is the heartbeat of any relationship. It's the rhythm that keeps connections alive and thriving. By understanding its importance and consciously nurturing it, we can foster relationships that not only last but also enrich our lives in immeasurable ways.

Setting Boundaries While Remaining Open

Setting boundaries while remaining open is a delicate dance, but it's essential for healthy relationships. Imagine boundaries as invisible lines we draw around ourselves to define what we're comfortable with and what's a no-go. These lines aren't meant to shut people out but to protect our well-being.

In relationships, it's natural to want to share and connect deeply with others. But, there's a difference between opening up and overextending ourselves. For instance, we might share personal stories with close friends but not with acquaintances. That's a boundary. Or, we might be okay lending a book but not our favorite dress. Another boundary right there!

Boundaries can be emotional, physical, intellectual, or even financial. They help us maintain our individuality and ensure we're not constantly swayed by others' needs or opinions. But here's the thing: while setting boundaries is crucial, it's equally important to remain open and receptive. It's about finding that sweet spot where we feel safe and respected but are also welcoming and understanding towards others.

Being open doesn't mean letting everyone in indiscriminately. It means being selective about who we let close, ensuring mutual respect. When we set clear boundaries, we signal to others how we want to be treated. And when these boundaries are respected, trust grows, paving the way for deeper, more meaningful connections.

Remember, it's okay to say no, to prioritize your well-being, and to ask for what you need. And it's equally okay to listen, understand, and respect others' boundaries. After all, in the dance of relationships, it's the balance between setting boundaries and remaining open that creates a harmonious rhythm.

Sub-chapter 4.3: Vulnerability in Professional Settings

Showing Humanity in Leadership

In today's fast-paced corporate world, leadership often gets equated with stoicism, unwavering determination, and an unemotional demeanor. However, a new wave of thought is challenging this archetype. The most impactful leaders today are those who show their humanity, embracing vulnerability as a strength rather than a weakness.

Imagine a CEO who openly shares their struggles, fears, and uncertainties with their team. Instead of perceiving them as weak, the team sees a leader who is relatable, genuine, and human. This authenticity fosters a deeper connection between the leader and their team, creating an environment of trust and mutual respect. When leaders remove their masks of invincibility, they pave the way for open communication, fostering a culture where employees feel safe to voice their concerns, share their ideas, and admit their mistakes.

Moreover, showing humanity in leadership isn't just about being open about one's feelings. It's about demonstrating empathy, actively listening, and genuinely caring about the well-being of team members. It's about recognizing that every individual, including the leader, is on a continuous journey of growth and learning.

In a study published in the Harvard Business Review, it was found that leaders who exhibited vulnerability were often rated higher in terms of trustworthiness and reliability by their subordinates. Their approachability made them more effective in their roles, as teams were more inclined to approach them with innovative ideas, concerns, or feedback.

In essence, by showing humanity, leaders are not diluting their authority but amplifying their influence. They are building bridges of trust and understanding, which are foundational for any successful organization. Embracing vulnerability in leadership is not about being weak; it's about being wise enough to recognize that in our shared human experience lies the power to inspire, connect, and lead with authenticity.

The Balance: Professionalism and Authenticity

In the professional world, there's a delicate dance between maintaining a polished, professional demeanor and showcasing genuine authenticity. For years, the corporate ladder seemed to favor the stoic, the unflappable, the ever-professional. But times are changing, and today's leaders are realizing the power of authenticity in fostering trust, building relationships, and driving results.

Professionalism has its merits, of course. It ensures consistency, sets standards, and provides a framework for expected behavior. It's the suit and tie, the polished presentation, the timely response to emails. But authenticity? That's the passion in a leader's voice, the admission of a mistake, the genuine laughter shared with a team.

Blending the two might seem like a challenge. After all, how can one be both professional and authentic without compromising one for the other? The key lies in understanding that professionalism doesn't mean being robotic or devoid of emotion. It means conducting oneself with integrity, respect, and competence. Authenticity, on the other hand, is about being true to oneself, acknowledging imperfections, and being genuine.

When leaders manage to intertwine these two qualities, magic happens. Teams feel more connected to their leaders, trust is built at a faster rate, and workplaces become more collaborative and innovative. Employees are more likely to rally behind a leader who they believe is genuine, who they feel truly understands and cares about them.

Incorporating authenticity into professionalism doesn't mean oversharing personal details or being inappropriately informal. It means showing up as your true self, being open to feedback, and being willing to connect on a human level. It's about recognizing that every individual, including leaders, is a mosaic of strengths, weaknesses, experiences, and emotions.

In the end, the most respected leaders aren't those who put on a perfect facade. They're the ones who, while maintaining professional standards, aren't afraid to show their human side. They understand that in the balance between professionalism and authenticity, it's not about choosing one over the other, but rather seamlessly blending the two to create a leadership style that's both effective and genuine.

Gaining Respect through Genuine Interactions

Gaining respect in professional settings often hinges on the authenticity of our interactions. In a world where superficiality can sometimes take center stage, genuine interactions stand out, creating lasting impressions and fostering trust.

Imagine walking into a meeting and, instead of the usual pleasantries, your colleague shares a genuine concern or a personal anecdote related to the project. This openness can break down walls, making room for more honest discussions and collaborative problem-solving. It's not about oversharing or making everything personal; it's about being real in the moments that count.

Authenticity in communication can be a game-changer. When team members feel they can be themselves and speak their truths without judgment, creativity flourishes. People are more likely to voice their ideas, concerns, and solutions, leading to richer discussions and better outcomes.

Moreover, genuine interactions can lead to stronger professional relationships. When you show interest in others, listen actively, and engage in meaningful conversations, you're not just networking; you're building connections. These connections can lead to collaborations, partnerships, and opportunities down the line.

In essence, to gain respect in any professional setting, it's crucial to be genuine. Authentic interactions show that you value others, not just for their professional contributions but for who they are as individuals. And in return, you'll find that people will value and respect you all the more for it.

Sub-chapter 4.4: The Healing Power of Sharing

Expressing Fears and Doubts

Life is a rollercoaster of emotions, and it's natural for all of us to experience fears and doubts. But have you ever noticed the weight that lifts off your shoulders when you share these feelings with someone you trust? There's a reason for that.

Expressing our fears and doubts is not just about venting. It's a process of externalizing our internal struggles, giving them a voice, and acknowledging their existence. When we keep our worries bottled up, they tend to magnify. They play on a loop in our minds, often becoming more daunting than they truly are.

Sharing these feelings does a couple of things. First, it allows us to see our concerns from a different perspective. When we put our fears into words, we often realize that they aren't as insurmountable as they seemed in our heads. Secondly, sharing creates a connection. The person listening can offer support, understanding, or even share their similar experiences. This mutual exchange reminds us that we're not alone in our struggles.

Moreover, expressing our doubts can lead to solutions. Discussing them can spark ideas, suggestions, or strategies that we hadn't considered before. It's like turning on a light in a dark room. Suddenly, things become clearer, and paths that were previously hidden come into view.

In a world that often values stoicism and "keeping it together," it's essential to remember that showing vulnerability by expressing our fears and doubts is a strength. It's a brave act that paves the way for healing, growth, and deeper connections with those around us. So, the next time you feel weighed down by worries, remember the power of sharing. It might just be the first step towards finding your way through the maze of uncertainty.

Finding Supportive Communities

Finding a supportive community can be a game-changer in our journey to embrace vulnerability. Imagine walking into a room and feeling like you've come home. That's the power of a supportive community. It's a space where you can be your authentic self, share your fears, dreams, and even your quirks, without the fear of judgment.

In today's digital age, many of us feel isolated despite being constantly connected. We scroll through social media, seeing curated versions of people's lives, and it's easy to feel like we're the only ones struggling. But here's the thing: everyone has their battles, and many are looking for genuine connections just like you.

Joining or creating a supportive community, be it a book club, a fitness group, or even a virtual forum centered around a shared interest or challenge, can provide that safe space to express and be understood. These communities become a mirror, reflecting our shared human experiences, making us feel less alone.

But how do you find your tribe? Start by identifying your interests or challenges. Attend local events or workshops, or explore online forums or groups. Remember, it's about quality, not quantity. A few genuine connections can be more enriching than a thousand acquaintances. And as you share and support others, you'll find that you're not only healing yourself but also contributing to the healing of others. It's a beautiful cycle of give and take, rooted in authenticity and mutual respect.

Testimonials: How Sharing Transformed Lives

The act of sharing personal experiences can be transformative, not just for the sharer but also for those who listen. Let's dive into a couple of stories that highlight this magic.

Meet Maya. After years of silently battling depression, she finally mustered the courage to share her journey at a local support group. The outpouring of empathy and understanding she received was overwhelming. But what truly surprised her was the number of people who approached her afterward, saying her story gave them the strength to seek help. By sharing, Maya not only found healing for herself but also became a beacon of hope for others.

Then there's Alex, who survived a traumatic accident. He began documenting his recovery on a blog, detailing the highs, the lows, and everything in between. His raw and honest account resonated with many, especially those facing their own physical challenges. Alex's blog became a community where people found solace in shared experiences. He often says, "In sharing, I found purpose. I realized my pain had a bigger role—it could inspire resilience in others."

These stories underscore a profound truth: our personal narratives have the power to heal, inspire, and connect. When we share, we not only lighten our own burdens but also illuminate paths for others.

Sub-chapter 4.5: The Daily Practice of Embracing Vulnerability

Journaling and Self-Reflection

Journaling isn't just about recording the events of the day; it's a deep dive into the soul, a conversation with oneself. It's where vulnerability meets paper, allowing us to confront our rawest emotions and thoughts head-on.

Imagine having a friend who's always there, ready to listen without judgment. That's what your journal can be. On days when doubt clouds your mind, pouring those feelings onto paper can be cathartic. It's like decluttering the mind, making space for clarity and understanding.

Self-reflection through journaling is also a powerful tool for growth. By revisiting past entries, you can track your emotional journey, recognize patterns, and celebrate how far you've come. It's like having a mirror that reflects not just your face, but your heart and soul.

And here's a little secret: vulnerability on paper often translates to strength in the real world. By acknowledging and understanding your fears and doubts, you're better equipped to face them outside the safe confines of your journal.

So, grab a notebook, find a quiet corner, and start writing. Let the words flow, uncensored and unfiltered. You might be surprised at the depth of insight and understanding that emerges from this simple daily practice.

Cultivating an Open Mindset

Cultivating an open mindset is like opening the windows of a stuffy room to let in fresh air. It's about allowing new ideas, experiences, and perspectives to flow freely into your life, refreshing your thoughts and broadening your horizons.

In a world that often encourages us to build walls around our beliefs and emotions, having an open mindset is a revolutionary act. It means being willing to listen, even when we don't agree. It means being curious about the world and the people in it, seeking to understand rather than judge.

But how do we cultivate this openness? It starts with self-awareness. Recognize when you're holding onto rigid beliefs and challenge them. Ask yourself, "Why do I feel this way? Is there another perspective I haven't considered?"

Next, expose yourself to diverse experiences. Read books from different cultures, engage in conversations with people from varied backgrounds, and be a lifelong learner. Embrace the unfamiliar, and let it enrich your understanding of the world.

Remember, an open mindset isn't about agreeing with everyone or abandoning your values. It's about being receptive, adaptable, and willing to grow. As the saying goes, "The mind is like a parachute; it works best when open."

Rituals to Connect

With

One's Inner Self

In the hustle and bustle of daily life, it's easy to lose touch with our inner selves. Yet, reconnecting with that core part of us can be the key to embracing vulnerability and living authentically. Here are some daily rituals to help you forge that connection:

1. Mindful Meditation: Start your day with a few minutes of meditation. Focus on your breath, the sensations in your body, and the present moment. This practice helps you tune into your feelings and thoughts without judgment.

2. Gratitude Journaling: Every evening, jot down three things you're grateful for. This simple act shifts your focus from what's lacking or overwhelming to what's abundant and beautiful in your life.

3. Nature Walks: Spend some time outdoors, even if it's just a short walk around

the block. Nature has a way of grounding us and reminding us of our place in the larger scheme of things.

4. Digital Detox: Dedicate an hour before bedtime to disconnect from screens. Use this time to read, listen to calming music, or simply sit in silence. It's a way to declutter your mind and prepare for restful sleep.

5. Deep Breathing Exercises: Whenever you feel overwhelmed, pause and take a few deep breaths. This calms the nervous system and brings clarity.

Remember, the journey inward is deeply personal. These rituals are starting points; feel free to adapt them to what resonates with you. Embracing vulnerability starts with understanding and honoring oneself.

Chapter Six

Building Resilience

The Cornerstone of Confidence

"Our greatest glory is not in never falling, but in rising every time we fall." – Confucius

In the ever-evolving journey of life, we're bound to face challenges, setbacks, and moments of doubt. But what if we told you that these very challenges could be the stepping stones to a more confident you? Enter resilience – the unsung hero of personal growth. Resilience isn't just about bouncing back; it's about growing through adversity, learning from experiences, and emerging stronger than before.

It's the inner fortitude that allows us to face life's storms head-on and say, "I've got this." This chapter delves deep into the art and science of building resilience, showcasing its pivotal role in fostering unwavering confidence. As we navigate through the subsequent sections, we'll uncover strategies, stories, and insights that illuminate the transformative power of resilience.

So, whether you're weathering a personal storm or simply looking to fortify your inner strength, this chapter serves as a beacon, guiding you toward a more resilient and confident self. Let's embark on this empowering journey together, discovering the incredible strength that lies within each of us.

Sub-chapter 5.1: Understanding Resilience

The Psychology Behind Bouncing Back

Resilience is often likened to a rubber band's ability to stretch and then snap back into its original shape. But in psychological terms, it's so much more than that. It's the intricate dance of the human spirit to face adversity, learn from it, and emerge even stronger.

Imagine facing a setback. It could be a job loss, a broken relationship, or any personal challenge. While the initial reaction might be despair or shock, the resilient mind starts to weave a different narrative. It begins to ask, "What can I learn from this?" instead of "Why did this happen to me?" This shift in perspective is pivotal. It's not about denying the pain or the challenge, but about harnessing it as a catalyst for growth.

Dr. Martin Seligman, often regarded as the father of positive psychology, has spoken about how resilience is not just an innate trait but can be developed. His research suggests that by understanding our personal explanatory styles (how we explain life's events to ourselves), we can foster resilience. It's about cultivating an optimistic outlook, even in the face of adversity.

In essence, resilience is the art of turning setbacks into comebacks. It's about understanding that life's challenges don't define us, but how we respond to them does. And with each challenge faced and overcome, our resilience muscle only grows stronger.

Resilience vs. Stubbornness

In our society, resilience is often hailed as a virtue. It's the ability to adapt, bounce back, and keep going despite challenges. On the other hand, stubbornness is seen as digging one's heels in, refusing to budge or adapt, even when it might be beneficial. But how do we distinguish between the two?

Linda O'Connell, in her reflection on LinkedIn, beautifully captures this distinction. She mentions, "If you adapt and persist, you are being resilient. If you don't adapt and continue persisting, you are just stubborn."

So, it's all about adaptability. Resilience involves recognizing when a change of approach is needed and then making that change. It's about learning from setbacks and using them as stepping stones. Stubbornness, in contrast, is about persisting without adapting. It's like trying to fit a square peg into a round hole over and over again.

Think of it like this: Imagine you're trying to reach the top of a mountain. A resilient person might try one path, face obstacles, then find another way up. A stubborn person would keep trying the same blocked path repeatedly, hoping it'll somehow clear up.

In life, as in the journey up that metaphorical mountain, it's essential to know when to persist and when to adapt. That's the key difference between resilience and mere stubbornness.

The Benefits of a Resilient Mindset

Hey there, ever wondered why some folks seem to bounce back from setbacks while others get bogged down? That's the magic of a resilient mindset! Let's dive into the perks of embracing this mindset.

1. Emotional Stability: Resilience helps you keep your cool. Instead of getting overwhelmed by emotions, you learn to process them, ensuring they don't dictate your reactions.

2. Growth from Adversity: Remember that old saying, "What doesn't kill you makes you stronger"? With resilience, you don't just survive challenges; you learn and grow from them.

3. Better Problem-Solving: Resilient individuals tend to see problems as puzzles waiting to be solved. They approach challenges with creativity and optimism.

4. Improved Relationships: When you're resilient, you're better equipped to handle interpersonal conflicts. You listen, understand, and communicate more effectively.

5. Enhanced Physical Health: Believe it or not, a resilient mindset can boost your immune system! Less stress means fewer stress-related illnesses.

6. Greater Life Satisfaction: Resilient folks often report a higher sense of contentment in life. They appreciate the highs and navigate the lows with grace.

7. Increased Persistence: With resilience, giving up isn't in the vocabulary. You're more likely to stick to your goals and see them through.

In a nutshell, a resilient mindset isn't just about bouncing back; it's about bouncing forward, better and stronger. So, next time life throws a curveball, remember the power of resilience and all the fantastic benefits it brings along!

Sub-chapter 5.2: Strategies to Enhance Resilience

Shifting Perspective on Failures

Failures, setbacks, and mistakes – we've all been there. But here's the thing: it's not the stumble that defines us, but how we rise after it. When we view failures as catastrophic events, we're setting ourselves up for a cycle of self-doubt and hesitation. But what if we could change that lens?

Imagine seeing failures as lessons, not losses. It's like going to school, but life is the teacher. Every mistake is a chapter in the textbook of personal growth. Instead of asking, "Why did this happen to me?", try "What can I learn from this?" This subtle shift in questioning can make a world of difference.

It's also essential to remember that everyone, from the most successful entrepreneur to the top athlete, has faced failures. But they didn't let those moments define them. They used them as stepping stones, not stumbling blocks.

By embracing this mindset, we not only build resilience but also open ourselves up to growth and innovation. After all, if Thomas Edison had given up after his first few attempts, we might still be in the dark. So, the next time you face a setback, take a deep breath, shift your perspective, and remember: it's just a lesson on the path to greatness. No quotes are needed, just some good old-fashioned encouragement!

The Power of Adaptability

In a world that's constantly changing, adaptability is no longer just a nice-to-have; it's a must-have. Adaptability is the ability to learn flexibly and efficiently, applying that knowledge across various situations. It's about learning how to learn and knowing when to activate that learning mindset. When we're adaptable, we're not just reacting to challenges; we're preparing for them and navigating them with grace.

Adaptability is crucial during transformative periods. It allows us to learn faster and better, focusing on future opportunities rather than just present challenges. However, there's an "adaptability paradox" where, during times when we most need to adapt and learn, we often revert to familiar patterns, potentially stifling innovation and growth.

Building adaptability isn't just about individual growth. It's about fostering an environment where adaptability thrives. Leaders play a pivotal role in this. By promoting adaptability as a core value, leaders can transform their relationship with change and uncertainty, benefiting both themselves and their organizations.

A few key takeaways:

1. Adaptability is a Meta-Skill: It's not just about learning a new skill but understanding how to learn and when to apply that learning.

2. The Adaptability Paradox: When change is most needed, we often revert to what we know, which can hinder growth.

3. Leadership's Role: Leaders must champion adaptability, fostering an environment where it's valued and practiced.

Adaptable organizations and individuals don't just survive; they thrive. In a world where the only constant is change, adaptability is the key to unlocking endless possibilities.

Building a Support System

Building a robust support system is like constructing a safety net beneath a tightrope walker. It's that assurance that if you fall, there's something or someone to catch you. The importance of social circumstances in resilience is often overlooked, but it plays a pivotal role. How resilient we are can be significantly influenced by our social environment and circle of support, including our communities, institutions, and cultural expectations.

Elliot Friedman, a resiliency researcher, emphasizes the significance of various forms of social support, such as emotional and instrumental support, in facing challenges. Positive social relationships are undeniably beneficial, leading to greater psychological and physical well-being. These relationships also play a crucial role in resilience, as they help alleviate stress during tough times. For instance, studies have shown that positive relationships at one stage of life can predict reduced depression later on. Especially for older adults, these relationships can be protective against declining cognitive abilities or health challenges.

The American Psychological Association highlights that caring and supportive relationships, both within and outside the family, are. Such relationships, which foster love, trust, and encouragement, significantly bolster an individual's resilience. So, when life throws curveballs, it's essential to lean on your social networks, whether they offer emotional support or a helping hand. As Friedman puts it, engaging in meaningful activities that benefit others has a significant social component, enhancing resilience.

Sub-chapter 5.3: Resilience in Everyday Challenges

Facing Daily Setbacks with Grace

Facing daily setbacks with grace is an art, and it's one that can be cultivated. Life, as we know, isn't a straight line. It's more like a roller coaster with its ups, downs, twists, and turns. And while we can't always control the ride, we can control our reactions to it.

Every day, we're met with challenges, both big and small. Maybe it's a spilled coffee in the morning, a missed deadline at work, or a disagreement with a loved one. These setbacks, though seemingly trivial, can pile up and weigh us down. But here's the thing: it's not the setback itself but our response to it that defines our day.

Resilient individuals have a knack for seeing setbacks as temporary and isolated events rather than pervasive and permanent. They don't let one bad moment dictate the rest of their day. Instead, they take a deep breath, assess the situation, and move forward with a positive attitude. It's like having an internal reset button.

But how do they do it? A lot of it comes down to perspective. They understand that setbacks are a natural part of life and that every challenge is an opportunity for growth. By reframing the situation and focusing on solutions rather than dwelling on the problem, they navigate through daily challenges with a sense of grace and poise.

So, the next time you face a setback, remember: it's just a moment in time. Take a step back, reframe, and move forward with grace. Your resilience muscle will thank you for it!

Building Mental Stamina

Building mental stamina is akin to strengthening a muscle; it requires consistent effort and the right strategies. One of the most potent ways to combat anxiety and bolster mental strength is through resilience. Neuroscientist Wendi Suzuki emphasizes the significance of viewing challenges with an optimistic lens. By visualizing positive outcomes, we can train our minds to expect favorable results, which can lead to proactive actions toward achieving those outcomes.

Another strategy is to transform anxiety into progress. Our brain's adaptability allows us to reframe our thoughts and make informed decisions. Emotions like anger, fear, sadness, worry, and frustration can either hinder us or propel us forward, depending on our perspective.

Trying new activities, even simple ones, can push our boundaries and introduce novel experiences that challenge our brains. Additionally, maintaining connections with loved ones and seeking support when needed can be a protective shield against overwhelming stress.

A unique approach is practicing "positive self-tweeting." Inspired by Lin-Manual Miranda, sending out positive affirmations or messages to oneself can set a positive tone for the day. Lastly, immersing oneself in nature can be a therapeutic way to reconnect with oneself and find tranquility.

Case Studies: Overcoming Minor to Major Challenges

Resilience isn't just about bouncing back from life-altering events; it's also about navigating the daily challenges that test our patience, determination, and spirit. Let's explore a few real-life examples that showcase resilience in action:

1. The Job Seeker: After facing multiple rejections in her job hunt, Maria didn't lose hope. Instead, she took a step back, honed her skills, and networked more effectively. Her persistence paid off when she landed her dream job a few months

later.

2. The Small Business Owner: Raj's cafe was hit hard during an economic down-
   turn. Instead of shutting down, he adapted by offering delivery services and
   hosting virtual events, turning potential failure into a thriving business.

3. The Student: Jake struggled with dyslexia, making reading a challenge. But
   with determination, he used audiobooks and other tools to excel in his studies,
   proving that challenges can be turned into strengths with the right mindset.

4. The Athlete: After a severe injury, Sofia was told she might never run again. But
   with rigorous physiotherapy and mental conditioning, she not only returned to
   the track but also set a personal best.

5. The Parent: Balancing work and parenting during a pandemic was tough for
   Liam. But he set boundaries, created a routine, and sought support, turning a
   challenging period into quality family time.

These stories remind us that resilience is about adapting, learning, and growing, no matter
the size of the challenge. It's the small victories, the minor adjustments, and the daily
decisions to keep going that truly define our strength.

Sub-chapter 5.4: Cultivating Emotional Intelligence

Understanding and Managing Emotions

Emotional intelligence (EI or EQ for "emotional quotient") is a fascinating facet of our
psyche that plays a pivotal role in how we perceive, interpret, and manage our emotions.
At its core, it's about understanding not just our own emotions, but also those of the
people around us. Think of it as a dance between expressing and controlling emotions
while also tuning into and responding to the emotions of others.

Now, let's dive a bit deeper. Have you ever met someone who just seems to 'get' people?
They can read a room, they're empathetic, and they handle tricky situations with grace.
That's emotional intelligence in action. Some experts even argue that EQ might be more
crucial than IQ in determining life success. Imagine that!

A few hallmarks of someone with high EQ include the ability to identify and describe feelings, a keen sense of self-awareness, and a knack for managing emotions, even in tough situations. It's not just about recognizing emotions; it's about understanding them. For instance, if someone's upset, an emotionally intelligent person will try to figure out why and how best to respond.

But here's the kicker: emotional intelligence isn't just something you're born with. It can be developed and honed over time. So, if you're looking to boost your EQ, start by listening more, empathizing with others, and reflecting on your own emotions. Remember, understanding and managing our emotions is a journey, not a destination. And it's a journey well worth taking.

Building Empathy

Empathy is that magical ability that allows us to recognize, understand, and share the thoughts and feelings of another person, animal, or even a fictional character. Think of it as a bridge that connects us to others, making our interactions more genuine and compassionate. It's not just about understanding someone else's perspective, but genuinely feeling it. This is what makes us humans so unique and special.

Empathy is like a muscle; the more we use it, the stronger it becomes. And it's essential for building relationships. When we truly empathize, we're not just nodding our heads; we're connecting on a deeper level. It's like saying, "I see you, I hear you, and I'm here for you."

But here's a little nugget of concern: some surveys suggest that empathy might be on a decline, especially in places like the United States. This is a wake-up call for all of us. We need to nurture and promote empathy, especially in our younger generations. After all, it's empathy that binds us together, fosters understanding, and makes the world a kinder place.

Empathy isn't just about feeling sad when someone else is sad. It's also about celebrating their joys and successes. In relationships, for instance, being empathetic during the good times can be as crucial as being there during the tough times. And guess what? Even those who might seem self-centered, like narcissists, have the capacity for empathy. It might be limited, but it's there.

However, like all good things, there's a balance to be struck. Being overly empathetic can sometimes blind us to our own needs. It's essential to care for others, but we shouldn't forget to care for ourselves in the process.

In a nutshell, empathy is the glue that holds society together. It's the soft power that can heal wounds, bridge divides, and bring about real change. So, let's cherish it, cultivate it, and spread it far and wide.

Emotional Regulation in High-Stress Situations

Emotional regulation in high-stress situations is akin to mastering the art of staying calm in the eye of a storm. It's about harnessing the ability to manage and respond to overwhelming emotions in a way that's constructive rather than destructive.

Imagine you're in a heated argument, and your heart rate is skyrocketing. Or perhaps you're about to give a major presentation, and your palms are sweaty. These are moments where emotional regulation is crucial. It's not about suppressing or ignoring your feelings but understanding them, giving them space, and choosing how to act on them.

Research has shown that individuals who can effectively regulate their emotions in tense situations tend to have better interpersonal relationships, higher self-esteem, and even better physical health. They're also less likely to engage in harmful behaviors like substance abuse or self-harm.

So, how can one cultivate this skill? It begins with self-awareness. Recognizing the early signs of emotional escalation allows you to take proactive steps. Deep breathing, for instance, can help activate the body's relaxation response. Grounding exercises, like focusing on the five senses, can also help divert attention from distressing emotions and bring you back to the present moment.

Another key strategy is cognitive reframing. This involves changing the narrative you tell yourself about a situation. Instead of thinking, "I can't handle this," you might say, "This is tough, but I've overcome challenges before."

Lastly, remember that it's okay to seek support. Whether it's talking to a trusted friend or seeking professional help, sometimes an external perspective can provide clarity and guidance. After all, emotional regulation is not about going it alone but leveraging all the tools and resources at your disposal to navigate life's ups and downs with grace and resilience.

Sub-chapter 5.5: Resilience-Boosting Exercises

Mindfulness and Meditation Practices

Mindfulness and meditation have emerged as powerful tools for cultivating resilience. At their core, these practices are about grounding oneself in the present moment, fostering a deep awareness of one's thoughts, emotions, and sensations without judgment.

Mindfulness is the act of paying attention to the present moment with an open and non-judgmental attitude. It's about observing your thoughts and feelings without getting caught up in them. Think of it as a mental pause button, allowing you to step back and view your experiences from a distance. This perspective shift can be invaluable, especially when faced with challenging situations, as it provides a buffer against impulsive reactions and fosters a calm, centered response.

Meditation, on the other hand, is a structured practice that often incorporates mindfulness but can also involve focused attention, visualization, or mantra repetition. Regular meditation has been shown to reduce stress, improve concentration, and boost overall well-being. It's like a workout for your brain, strengthening neural pathways associated with positive emotions and resilience.

Incorporating these practices into your daily routine doesn't require hours of silent contemplation. Even just a few minutes of focused breathing or a short guided meditation can make a significant difference. Over time, these moments of mindfulness can accumulate, leading to a more resilient and balanced state of mind.

For those interested in diving deeper, numerous resources, apps, and courses are available to guide you on your mindfulness journey. Remember, it's not about achieving a state of perpetual calm but rather about cultivating an awareness that allows you to navigate life's ups and downs with grace and poise.

Challenging Oneself Regularly

Challenging oneself regularly is akin to flexing a muscle; the more you do it, the stronger and more resilient it becomes. It's a principle that's deeply rooted in our evolutionary history. Our ancestors faced numerous challenges, from hunting for food to surviving harsh climates. Those who adapted and overcame these challenges passed on their resilient genes to future generations.

In today's world, we might not be hunting for our next meal, but we still face challenges, both big and small. Whether it's taking on a new project at work, learning a new skill, or even facing our fears, these challenges push us out of our comfort zones. And it's outside this comfort zone where growth happens.

When you challenge yourself, you're essentially training your brain to handle stress and adversity. It's like building a mental resilience muscle. Each time you face a challenge and come out on the other side, you're reinforcing the idea that you can handle adversity. This not only boosts your self-confidence but also prepares you for future challenges.

Moreover, challenging oneself has been linked to increased creativity, problem-solving skills, and even improved mental health. It's a way of telling yourself, "I got this," no matter what life throws your way.

So, the next time you're faced with a challenge, embrace it. See it as an opportunity to grow, learn, and become a more resilient version of yourself. Remember, it's not about how many times you fall, but how many times you get back up. And each challenge, no matter how big or small, is an opportunity to rise even higher.

Adopting a Growth Mindset

Have you ever heard someone say, "I'm just not a math person" or "I'm not creative at all"? These are classic examples of a fixed mindset, where individuals believe their abilities are static and unchangeable. But here's the game-changer: the growth mindset. This perspective, popularized by Dr. Carol Dweck, suggests that abilities and intelligence can be developed through dedication, hard work, and, most importantly, a love for learning.

Imagine viewing challenges as opportunities rather than threats. With a growth mindset, failures aren't the end; they're just stepping stones to success. It's like turning on a switch in your brain that says, "I can learn and improve." This mindset doesn't just apply to academics or work; it's a life philosophy. Whether you're picking up a new hobby, navigating relationships, or facing personal hurdles, seeing the potential for growth can be transformative.

So, how do you cultivate this mindset? Start by embracing challenges, persisting in the face of setbacks, and understanding that effort is a path to mastery. Remember, feedback is constructive, not criticism. Surround yourself with people who uplift and challenge you. And most importantly, celebrate the journey of learning, not just the end result.

By adopting a growth mindset, you're not just enhancing your abilities; you're setting yourself up for a lifetime of learning and personal development. And trust me, that's a journey worth embarking on.

Chapter Seven

The Role of Physical Health in Confidence Building

"To keep the body in good health is a duty, otherwise we shall not be able to keep our mind strong and clear." – Buddha

In the intricate dance of life, our physical health and confidence are partners, each influencing the rhythm of the other. It's a relationship that's often overlooked, but the harmony between our body's well-being and our self-assurance is undeniable. This chapter delves into the profound connection between the vitality of our body and the strength of our self-belief.

When we nourish our bodies, engage in regular physical activity, and prioritize our health, we're not just investing in our physical future; we're also bolstering our mental fortitude. A healthy body often translates to a clearer mind, elevated moods, and, you guessed it, heightened confidence. As we journey through this chapter, we'll explore the science behind this connection, understand the transformative power of simple health habits, and discover actionable steps to merge physical health with confidence-building.

Whether you're a fitness enthusiast or someone just starting their health journey, this chapter offers insights and encouragement to intertwine physical well-being with the growth of self-assurance. Let's embark on this enlightening journey, understanding that every step we take towards our physical health is also a stride towards a more confident self.

Sub-chapter 6.1: Exercise and Mental Well-Being

The Brain-Endorphin Connection

Ever wondered why after a good workout, despite the sweat and exhaustion, you feel invigorated and happy? That's the magic of endorphins at play! Endorphins are chemicals produced by our brain in response to stress or pain. Think of them as our body's natural painkillers. When we exercise, especially during high-intensity workouts, our body perceives it as a form of stress. In response, our brain releases a higher amount of these feel-good chemicals.

But it's not just about feeling good in the moment. Regular exercise and the consequent endorphin release can have long-term benefits for our mental well-being. It can help reduce symptoms of depression and anxiety, improve mood, and even boost self-esteem. The more you engage in physical activity, the more you're equipping your brain to handle stress better.

So, the next time you're feeling down or stressed, remember the power of exercise. Not only will you be taking care of your physical health, but you'll also be giving your brain a delightful endorphin boost!

Routine Exercises for Mood Elevation

Ever had one of those days where you're feeling a bit down, and someone suggests, "Hey, why not go for a run?" And you think, "Run? I can barely walk to the fridge." But here's the thing: they might be onto something. Exercise isn't just about getting those abs or running a marathon. It's a secret weapon against the blues.

A brisk walk in the park can be a game-changer. The fresh air, the chirping birds, and the rhythmic pace of your steps can work wonders. It's like nature's own therapy session. And if you're more of an indoor person, dancing can be your go-to. Put on your favorite tunes and dance like no one's watching. It's not just fun; it's a mood elevator.

Yoga is another fantastic option. Those stretches and poses aren't just good for flexibility; they help in grounding and centering your mind. The deep breaths you take during yoga send a message to your brain to relax and stay calm.

Lastly, if you're up for a challenge, try high-intensity interval training (HIIT). It's short, it's intense, and it releases a flood of endorphins, the body's feel-good chemicals.

So, the next time you're feeling a bit off, remember: movement is magic. Whether it's a walk, a dance, or a yoga pose, your mood will thank you for it.

The Link Between Stamina and Self-Assurance

Ever noticed how after a long run or an intense workout session, you feel like you can conquer the world? That's not just the endorphins talking. Stamina, or the ability to sustain prolonged physical or mental effort, plays a pivotal role in boosting our self-assurance.

Building stamina isn't just about physical endurance; it's a testament to our mental fortitude. Every time we push our limits, whether it's running that extra mile or holding a plank for a few more seconds, we're sending a powerful message to our brain: "I can do this." This repeated affirmation strengthens our belief in our capabilities.

Moreover, as we see progress in our stamina, it becomes a tangible metric of our growth and perseverance. This progress acts as a confidence booster. Think about it: if you can push through the pain and fatigue of a workout, what's stopping you from facing life's challenges head-on?

Additionally, the discipline and commitment required to build stamina spill over into other areas of our lives. It teaches us the value of persistence, patience, and hard work. Over time, as our stamina improves, so does our self-assurance. We begin to trust ourselves more, knowing that we have the resilience and strength to overcome obstacles, both physical and mental.

In essence, stamina is more than just physical endurance; it's a cornerstone of our self-confidence. So, the next time you're pushing your limits, remember: you're not just building muscle; you're building self-assurance.

Sub-chapter 6.2: Nutrition and Mind Health

Foods that Boost Cognitive Function

Ever had a day where your brain feels foggy, and you can't remember where you left your keys? Well, the foods you eat can play a significant role in keeping your brain sharp. Here's a quick rundown of some brain-boosting foods:

1. Fatty Fish: Think salmon, trout, and sardines. These fish are loaded with omega-3 fatty acids, which are essential for brain health. About 60% of our brain is fat, and half of that is omega-3s. These fats are crucial for learning, memory, and even mood. Plus, they might help slow down age-related mental decline.

2. Blueberries: These little berries are antioxidant powerhouses. They can help improve communication between brain cells and might even enhance memory and cognitive processes.

3. Turmeric: This vibrant yellow spice contains curcumin, which can cross the blood-brain barrier. It's been linked to improved memory, mood, and even the growth of new brain cells.

4. Broccoli: Packed with antioxidants and vitamin K, broccoli can help protect the brain from damage and support cognitive health.

5. Pumpkin Seeds: These seeds are rich in magnesium, iron, zinc, and copper. All these nutrients play a role in brain health, from nerve signaling to regulating brain function.

6. Dark Chocolate: Not only is it delicious, but dark chocolate (with 70% or more cocoa) also contains flavonoids, caffeine, and antioxidants. These compounds might help improve memory and even boost mood.

7. Nuts: Especially walnuts, which contain omega-3 fatty acids. Nuts are also rich in antioxidants and vitamin E, which can protect the brain from free-radical damage.

8. Oranges: High in vitamin C, oranges can help defend the brain against damage from free radicals.

9. Eggs: They're a good source of choline, which is crucial for mood and memory regulation.

10. Green Tea: It contains caffeine and L-theanine, which can improve alertness, performance, and focus.

Incorporating these foods into your diet can help support brain health and boost your cognitive functions. So, the next time you're feeling a bit sluggish, maybe reach for a handful of blueberries or a cup of green tea!

The Impact of Diet on Mood and Self-Perception

Ever had a sugar rush and then a subsequent crash? That's a simple example of how what we eat can directly affect our mood. But it's not just sugar; our entire diet plays a role in how we feel about ourselves and the world around us.

Research has shown that certain foods can boost our mood. For instance, foods rich in omega-3 fatty acids, like salmon, can help combat depression. On the flip side, a diet high in processed foods and sugars can increase the risk of depression and anxiety. It's not just about the immediate effects; over time, consistently poor dietary choices can lead to chronic mood disorders.

Moreover, our self-perception is closely tied to our diet. Ever noticed how you feel more confident and positive about yourself when you're making healthier food choices? That's because, deep down, we associate good nutrition with self-care and self-worth. When we nourish our bodies with the right foods, we're sending a message to our brains that we value ourselves.

In contrast, constantly indulging in junk food can lead to feelings of guilt and low self-worth. It's a vicious cycle: you eat poorly, feel bad about yourself, then eat poorly again to cope with those feelings.

In essence, our diet is a reflection of how we feel about ourselves. By making mindful, healthy choices, we can boost our mood, improve our self-perception, and set ourselves up for a more confident, positive life. Remember, you are what you eat, so choose foods that reflect the best version of you!

Incorporating a Balanced Diet for Optimal Mental Health

When we think of diets, we often think of our physical health, like losing weight or building muscle. But did you know that what you eat can significantly impact your mental health too? It's not just about the number on the scale; it's about how you feel inside.

Our brain, like any other organ, requires essential nutrients to function optimally. A balanced diet, rich in fruits, vegetables, whole grains, lean proteins, and healthy fats, can provide these necessary nutrients. These foods are packed with vitamins, minerals, and antioxidants that help protect the brain and keep it functioning smoothly.

For instance, omega-3 fatty acids, found in fish and flaxseeds, are known to reduce inflammation and promote brain health. Foods rich in antioxidants, like berries and nuts, protect our brain from oxidative stress. Moreover, complex carbohydrates in whole grains provide a steady source of energy, ensuring our brain has the fuel it needs to think clearly and make decisions.

On the flip side, a diet high in processed foods, sugars, and unhealthy fats can lead to mood swings, fatigue, and even depression. It's like feeding your car the wrong type of fuel; it's not going to run efficiently.

Incorporating a balanced diet isn't just about physical health; it's a commitment to your mental well-being. So, the next time you're planning your meals, think of it as nourishing both your body and mind. After all, a happy brain leads to a confident you!

Sub-chapter 6.3: Sleep's Role in Confidence

The Rejuvenating Power of Rest

Ah, sleep. It's that magical realm where we escape the hustle and bustle of daily life, diving into dreams and waking up refreshed (well, ideally!). But did you know that a good night's sleep does more than just banish those pesky under-eye circles? It's a powerful rejuvenator for our minds and bodies.

When we sleep, our brains go into overdrive, processing the day's events, forming memories, and repairing neural pathways. It's like a nightly maintenance check for our minds.

Without this essential downtime, our cognitive functions can take a hit. We might struggle with decision-making, problem-solving, or even regulating our emotions.

Moreover, consistent restful sleep can boost our mood and overall well-being. Ever noticed how everything seems a bit brighter and challenges more manageable after a solid night's rest? That's not just your imagination. Sleep has a direct impact on our mental health, reducing stress, anxiety, and even depressive symptoms.

On the flip side, chronic sleep deprivation can erode our self-confidence. When we're constantly tired, it's hard to feel good about ourselves or our abilities. So, if you're aiming to boost your confidence, don't underestimate the power of catching those Z's. Prioritize sleep, and you'll be investing in a more confident, rejuvenated you. Remember, a well-rested mind is a confident one!

Sleep's Role in Decision-Making and Clarity

Ever had one of those days where every choice feels like a mountain to climb? It might just be because you didn't catch enough Z's the night before. Sleep isn't just about recharging our bodies; it's crucial for our brain's functionality, especially when it comes to making decisions.

During a good night's sleep, our brain goes through various stages, including the all-important REM (Rapid Eye Movement) stage. This is the time when our brain processes and consolidates memories, sorts out the day's events, and prepares us for the challenges ahead. When we're deprived of sleep, this process gets disrupted, leading to foggy thinking and indecisiveness.

Imagine your brain as a computer. Just as a computer needs regular updates and restarts to function optimally, our brains need sleep to process information, weigh pros and cons, and come to logical conclusions. Without adequate sleep, our brain's "software" can become glitchy, making it harder to choose the salad over the pizza or decide on a course of action at work.

So, the next time you're faced with a big decision, consider your sleep schedule. A well-rested mind is clearer, sharper, and more decisive. Remember, quality sleep isn't a luxury; it's a necessity for sound decision-making.

Creating a Sleep Routine for Consistent Energy

Creating a consistent sleep routine is like setting the stage for a grand performance every day. Imagine waking up, feeling like you've just had the most rejuvenating spa treatment, and you're ready to conquer the world. That's the magic of a good night's sleep.

Now, let's talk about the foundation of this routine. Your bedroom should be a sanctuary. Investing in a comfortable mattress and bedding is crucial. Think of it as a long-term investment in your well-being. And those blackout curtains? They're not just for fancy hotels. They ensure that external light doesn't mess with your sleep cycle. Speaking of light, the blue light from our devices can be a sleep-stealer. It's a good idea to disconnect at least an hour before bedtime. Let's give those scrolling fingers a rest!

But it's not just about the setup. It's also about the ritual. Setting a consistent bedtime and wake-up time, even on weekends, helps regulate your body's internal clock. And if you find yourself tossing and turning, don't watch the clock. Get up, do something relaxing, and return to bed when you feel sleepy.

Lastly, remember that what you eat and drink matters. Avoiding caffeine and heavy meals before bedtime can make a significant difference. And if you're still struggling, consider keeping a sleep diary. It can offer insights into patterns that might be affecting your sleep.

Remember, every good day starts the night before. So, let's prioritize our sleep and set the stage for success every day!

Sub-chapter 6.4: Physical Appearance and Self-Esteem

Decoding the Link: How Appearance Affects Confidence

Have you ever noticed how you feel a tad bit more confident when you're wearing your favorite outfit? Or perhaps a bit more self-conscious when you have a bad hair day? It's not just in your head; there's a genuine connection between our physical appearance and our self-esteem.

Our appearance, whether we like it or not, sends out signals to others about who we are. It's like a non-verbal introduction before we even speak. When we feel good about how we look, it often translates into feeling more confident in our interactions. This doesn't mean we need to adhere to societal standards of beauty, but rather find what makes us feel authentically good.

Research has shown that our self-perception, which includes how we view our physical appearance, can significantly impact our confidence levels. When we're content with our appearance, we're more likely to engage in social situations, take risks, and even perform better in tasks.

However, it's essential to strike a balance. While it's natural to want to look our best, it's equally crucial to understand that our worth isn't solely tied to our appearance. Confidence should come from a blend of how we feel inside and out. After all, true beauty radiates from within, and when we feel good on the inside, it shows on the outside. So, the next time you dress up or groom yourself, remember it's not just about looking good but feeling good too!

Dressing For Success: Fact or Fiction?

"Dressing for success: Fact or fiction?" It's a question that's been debated for years. Let's dive in, shall we?

When you hear "dress for success," you might picture sharp suits, polished shoes, and power ties. But is there more to it than just looking the part? Absolutely! Dressing well isn't just about impressing others; it's about how it makes you feel. When you wear clothes that fit well and reflect your personal style, it can give you a confidence boost. It's like putting on armor to face the world.

Research has shown that our attire can influence our thoughts and negotiations. For instance, wearing formal clothes can make people think more broadly and holistically. On the flip side, casual wear might make you feel more relaxed and creative.

But here's the catch: it's not a one-size-fits-all approach. What makes one person feel empowered might make another feel out of place. The key is authenticity. If you're wearing something just because it's "in" but doesn't resonate with you, it might do more harm than good.

In conclusion, while dressing well can certainly give you an edge in certain situations, it's essential to find a balance. Wear what makes you feel confident and authentic, and you'll be on the right track. Remember, it's not just about the clothes; it's about the person wearing them. So, is dressing for success a fact? Yes, but with a sprinkle of personal touch!

Balancing Self-Expression and Societal Norms

Balancing self-expression and societal norms is a dance many of us engage in daily. On one hand, we have this innate desire to showcase our unique personalities, beliefs, and values. It's a way of saying, "Hey, this is me!" On the other, there's the weight of societal expectations, which can sometimes feel like a heavy cloak, dictating how we should look, behave, and even think.

Self-expression is a beautiful thing. It's a reflection of our innermost thoughts, feelings, and experiences. When we express ourselves authentically, it can be incredibly empowering. It's like planting our flag in the world and declaring our individuality. But here's the catch: society, with its unwritten rules and standards, often has a say in how we "should" present ourselves.

Now, societal norms aren't all bad. They provide a framework that helps maintain order and predictability. But when these norms stifle our true selves, it can lead to feelings of dissatisfaction and even resentment.

So, how do we strike a balance? It's about finding that sweet spot where we feel true to ourselves while still navigating societal expectations. It might mean wearing that bold outfit to work but pairing it with more subdued accessories. Or speaking our mind but doing so with tact and respect for others. Remember, it's not about conforming or rebelling, but harmonizing our inner voice with the world around us.

Sub-chapter 6.5: Consistent Self-Care Rituals

The Importance of Taking Time for Oneself

In today's fast-paced world, it's easy to get caught up in the whirlwind of tasks, responsibilities, and social engagements. Amidst all this hustle, taking time for oneself often takes a backseat. But here's the thing: pausing and giving yourself a breather isn't just a luxury—it's essential.

Imagine your mind as a smartphone. Just as our devices need regular charging, our minds and souls need rejuvenation. Without it, we risk burnout, decreased productivity, and a dip in our overall well-being. Taking time for oneself is like hitting the refresh button, allowing us to bounce back with renewed energy and perspective.

Now, you might think, "I'm too busy for a break!" But self-care doesn't always mean a spa day or a weekend getaway (though those are lovely!). It can be as simple as a 10-minute meditation session, reading a few pages of a book, or even just sipping your morning coffee in silence.

By prioritizing ourselves, we're not being selfish. We're ensuring that we can show up as our best selves in every aspect of our lives. As the saying goes, "You can't pour from an empty cup." So, let's make a pact to regularly refill our cups and recognize the importance of taking time for oneself. It's not just beneficial—it's vital.

Self-Care Activities for Rejuvenation

When we talk about self-care, it's not just bubble baths and face masks—though they're pretty awesome. It's about activities that refuel us, rather than take from us.

1. Nature Walks: There's something magical about being outdoors. The fresh air, the chirping birds—it's nature's way of giving us a gentle hug. Even a short walk can clear the mind and boost our mood.

2. Journaling: Pouring your thoughts onto paper can be therapeutic. It's like having a conversation with yourself, understanding your feelings, and decluttering your mind.

3. Crafting: Ever tried knitting, painting, or even pottery? Engaging in creative activities can be incredibly soothing. Plus, you get a cool DIY souvenir at the end!

4. Listening to Music or Podcasts: Whether it's groovy beats or a calming podcast, immersing yourself in audio can be a delightful escape.

5. Mindful Breathing: Just a few minutes of focused breathing can center you. It's like a mini-vacation for your brain.

6. Cooking: Whipping up a meal, especially comfort food, can be both fun and rewarding. And the best part? You get to eat it!

Remember, self-care is deeply personal. What works for one might not work for another. The key is to find what resonates with you and make it a regular part of your routine. After all, you deserve it!

Setting Boundaries for Mental Well-Being

Ever felt drained after a long call with a friend who only talks about their problems? Or found yourself working late hours because you couldn't say no? That's where boundaries come into play.

1. Learn to Say "No": It's a small word, but oh-so-powerful. You don't have to attend every event or take on every task. It's okay to decline if it doesn't align with your well-being.

2. Limit Digital Intake: Constant notifications can be overwhelming. Designate tech-free times or use apps that limit social media usage. Your brain will thank you!

3. Protect Your Personal Time: Just as you schedule meetings, schedule "me-time". Whether it's reading, meditating, or just lounging—this time is sacred.

4. Communicate Clearly: If someone oversteps, communicate your feelings. It's not about confrontation but about mutual respect.

5. Re-evaluate Relationships: If someone consistently drains your energy, it might be time to reconsider the role they play in your life.

Remember, setting boundaries is a form of self-care. It's about ensuring you have the mental and emotional space to be your best self. As the saying goes, "You can't pour from an empty cup." So, keep your cup full and flourishing!

Chapter Eight

Social Dynamics and Navigating Relationships with Confidence

"We are born in relationship, we are wounded in relationship, and we can be healed in relationship." – Harville Hendrix

Navigating the intricate maze of social dynamics can often feel like tightrope walking. One misstep, and our confidence can take a tumble. But what if we told you that with the right tools and mindset, this tightrope can feel as wide as a sidewalk? This chapter dives deep into the world of relationships, from fleeting interactions to lifelong bonds, and how they shape our self-worth.

We'll explore the dance of give-and-take, the art of assertive communication, and the joy of genuine connections. Whether it's the workplace, family gatherings, or social outings, confidence plays a pivotal role in how we present ourselves and how others perceive us. But remember, it's not about wearing a mask of invulnerability; it's about understanding and embracing our authentic selves in every interaction. So, let's embark on this journey together, discovering how to navigate relationships with grace, empathy, and, most importantly, confidence.

Sub-chapter 7.1: Understanding Social Hierarchies

Decoding the Unspoken Rules

Ever walked into a room and felt an invisible tug, pulling you towards certain individuals and away from others? That's the silent dance of social hierarchies at play. These unspoken rules, often rooted in our evolutionary past, dictate a lot about our interactions. They're like the background music in a movie scene – you might not always notice it, but it sets the tone.

Now, these hierarchies aren't about dominance or submission, but more about understanding roles and dynamics. For instance, in a workplace, there's an unspoken respect for experience and position. In a group of friends, there might be the 'planner' everyone turns to for organizing hangouts. Recognizing these roles helps us navigate social situations more smoothly.

But here's the golden nugget: while it's essential to understand these rules, it's equally crucial not to be bound by them. The most magnetic individuals often dance to their own rhythm, even while being aware of the background music. So, as you step into different social arenas, take a moment to tune into these silent cues. They're your roadmap to more meaningful and confident interactions. And remember, it's always okay to add your own notes to the symphony!

Navigating Various Social Settings

Ah, the intricate dance of social settings! From casual coffee meetups to formal boardroom discussions, each setting has its own rhythm, and knowing how to move within them can feel like mastering different dance styles.

Let's start with casual settings, like a friend's barbecue or a local book club. Here, the vibe is relaxed. The key? Be yourself, listen actively, and share a bit of your world. It's like a freestyle dance – go with the flow and enjoy the moment.

Now, shift to a professional setting, say, a networking event. The atmosphere is more structured, like a waltz. Maintain eye contact, offer a firm handshake, and have your elevator pitch ready. Remember, it's about building connections, not just exchanging business cards.

Lastly, consider those tricky, ambiguous settings – maybe a friend's wedding where you only know the bride. Think of it as a salsa dance: vibrant and unpredictable. Start with small talk, find common ground, and soon enough, you'll be mingling like a pro.

In all these settings, confidence is your best accessory. Wear it proudly, and remember that every interaction is a chance to learn, grow, and shine. And hey, even if you miss a step, it's all part of the dance!

Elevating One's Status Without Diminishing Others

Navigating the social ladder can sometimes feel like a tightrope walk. You want to climb, but not at the expense of others. So, how do you elevate your status gracefully? Let's dive in.

Firstly, focus on self-improvement. Whether it's acquiring a new skill, expanding your knowledge, or simply being the best version of yourself, personal growth naturally elevates your status. And guess what? It's contagious! When you grow, you inspire those around you to do the same.

Next, practice active listening. It's a subtle art that makes a world of difference. By genuinely listening to others, you not only gain insights but also make the other person feel valued. It's a win-win!

Celebrate others' achievements. Instead of seeing someone else's success as a threat, view it as a collective win. By genuinely applauding others, you create an environment of mutual respect and admiration.

Lastly, lead with kindness and humility. A true leader isn't someone who stands above others but one who uplifts everyone around them. Remember, it's not about being the loudest in the room but the most impactful.

In essence, elevating your status is about growing together, not apart. It's about creating a ripple effect of positivity and growth. And in this journey, everyone's a winner!

Sub-chapter 7.2: Cultivating Meaningful Connections

Building Trust and Rapport

Ah, trust and rapport, the secret ingredients to any lasting relationship! Whether it's a budding friendship, a new colleague, or a neighbor across the hall, these two elements are the foundation of genuine connections. Let's break it down, shall we?

Trust isn't built overnight. It's like a plant that needs consistent care. Start with honesty. Be genuine in your interactions, even if it means showing vulnerability. People appreciate authenticity, and it's often reciprocated with trust.

Active listening is another golden ticket. When you truly listen to someone, you're saying, "I value you and what you have to say." It's a simple yet powerful gesture that fosters trust.

Now, onto rapport. Think of it as the melody that makes conversations flow. It's about finding common ground, shared interests, or even shared experiences. A great way to build rapport? Share a story or a light-hearted anecdote. It can be a bridge to deeper conversations.

Remember, body language speaks volumes. A warm smile, open posture, and maintaining eye contact can work wonders in building rapport.

In the grand tapestry of relationships, trust and rapport are the threads that hold everything together. So, invest time in them, nurture them, and watch your connections flourish.

Deep Listening and Mutual Respect

Ever been in a conversation where you felt truly heard? It's like a warm hug for the soul, isn't it? That's the magic of deep listening. It's not just about hearing words; it's about tuning into emotions, understanding context, and genuinely engaging with the person speaking.

Imagine you're tuning into a radio frequency. With deep listening, you're not just catching the main broadcast; you're also picking up on the subtle undertones, the emotions, and the unsaid words. It's an art, really. And the best part? When you deeply listen, you're silently telling the other person, "You matter to me."

Now, let's chat about mutual respect. It's the unsung hero in any meaningful connection. It's about valuing differences, acknowledging boundaries, and treating others how you'd like to be treated. Simple in theory, but oh-so-powerful in practice.

Combine deep listening with mutual respect, and you've got a recipe for connections that aren't just surface-level. These are the bonds that stand the test of time, weathering storms and celebrating sunny days.

So, next time you're in a conversation, try tuning in a little deeper, showing that respect a little more overtly. You might just be surprised at the depth of connection you can achieve.

Creating Lasting Bonds

Hey there, friend! Let's have a heart-to-heart about something we all crave: lasting connections. You know, the kind where you can pick up right where you left off, even if it's been ages? Those bonds that feel like a cozy blanket on a chilly night.

First off, lasting bonds aren't built overnight. They're like plants; they need time, care, and a sprinkle of patience. It's about showing up, being present, and genuinely investing in the relationship. It's not just about the big moments, but also the small, everyday interactions that weave the fabric of a deep connection.

Remember those late-night chats, the shared laughs, the times you stood by each other during tough patches? That's the stuff lasting bonds are made of. It's about vulnerability, trust, and mutual growth.

And here's a little secret: consistency is key. It's like watering that plant we talked about. Regular check-ins, understanding, and support can make all the difference.

So, if you're looking to create bonds that stand the test of time, be genuine, be there, and let the relationship evolve naturally. Because, in the end, it's the authentic, heartfelt connections that truly last a lifetime.

Sub-chapter 7.3: Setting and Enforcing Boundaries

The Importance of Personal Space

Hey there! Let's chat about something we all need but sometimes forget to prioritize: personal space. Think of it as your own little bubble, a sanctuary where you can breathe, think, and just be you.

Now, personal space isn't just about physical distance. It's also about emotional and mental space. Ever had one of those days where you just needed a moment to yourself? That's your inner self craving some personal space.

Here's the deal: Respecting our own boundaries and those of others is crucial for healthy relationships. It allows us to recharge, process our feelings, and come back to interactions with a clearer mind. Plus, when we have our own space, we can better appreciate the times we share with others.

But, why is personal space so essential? Well, it's tied to our sense of autonomy and self-respect. By setting boundaries, we're saying, "Hey, I value myself and my well-being."

So, the next time you feel overwhelmed or just need a breather, remember it's okay to take a step back and enjoy your personal space. It's not only beneficial for you but also for the relationships you cherish.

Communicating One's Needs Clearly

Alright, let's dive into a topic that many of us find a tad tricky: communicating our needs. Ever found yourself in a situation where you wished someone just understood what you wanted without you saying it? Yep, we've all been there. But here's the thing: mind-reading isn't a common skill, so it's up to us to make our needs known.

First off, it's essential to recognize that it's perfectly okay to have needs and desires. They're a part of being human. The key is to express them in a way that's both respectful and clear.

Start with "I" statements. Instead of saying, "You never listen to me," try, "I feel unheard when we discuss this topic." It's less accusatory and opens the door for understanding.

Also, be specific. If you need some alone time, instead of vaguely saying, "I need space," you might say, "I'd love to have an hour in the evenings to unwind by myself."

Remember, it's not just about what you say, but how you say it. A calm tone and open body language can make a world of difference.

In the end, clear communication is a two-way street. While we express our needs, it's equally important to listen and understand the needs of others. Mutual respect goes a long way.

The Link Between Respect and Boundary-Setting

Let's chat about something that's foundational in all our relationships: respect. Now, you might be wondering, "What's the connection between respect and setting boundaries?" Well, they're like two peas in a pod, intertwined and essential for healthy interactions.

When we set boundaries, we're essentially communicating our values, needs, and limits. It's like drawing a line in the sand and saying, "This is where I stand." And when others acknowledge and honor those boundaries, it's a clear sign of respect. It shows they value our feelings and well-being.

On the flip side, when we respect others, we're more attuned to their boundaries. We listen, understand, and avoid crossing lines that shouldn't be crossed. It's a mutual dance of give and take.

But here's a golden nugget: setting boundaries isn't just about saying "no" or keeping people at arm's length. It's about creating a safe space where relationships can flourish without the fear of overstepping or feeling overwhelmed.

In essence, boundaries are a testament to the respect we have for ourselves and others. They ensure that every interaction is rooted in understanding and mutual regard. So, the next time you set a boundary, remember it's not just a limit; it's a bridge to deeper respect.

Sub-chapter 7.4: Overcoming Social Anxiety

Recognizing Signs of Anxiety

Hey there, ever walked into a room and felt like everyone's eyes were on you? Or maybe you've had that sinking feeling in your stomach before a presentation? Welcome to the world of social anxiety. It's more common than you might think, and the first step to managing it is recognizing its signs.

When anxiety strikes, your heart might race like it's trying to win a marathon. Your palms could get all sweaty, and you might feel a bit shaky or dizzy. Some folks even feel nauseous. Mentally, it's like a whirlwind of thoughts, often negative, swirling around, making it hard to focus. You might start to doubt yourself, overthink your actions, or replay conversations in your head, wishing you'd said something different.

And then there's the urge to escape. Ever felt that? Like you just want to be anywhere but in that social setting? That's anxiety waving its not-so-friendly hand.

Many people experience these symptoms but brush them off as mere 'nervousness'. But understanding these as signs of social anxiety is crucial. Recognizing them means you're already on the path to managing and overcoming those anxious feelings. Remember, you're not alone in this, and there's a whole community out there ready to support and guide you.

Techniques to Remain Calm and Present

Hey, friend! So, you've recognized those pesky signs of social anxiety. Now, let's chat about some cool techniques to help you stay calm and in the moment. Trust me, with a little practice, you can be the master of your own mind.

First up, deep breathing. It sounds simple, but it's a game-changer. When anxiety hits, our breathing gets shallow. Taking slow, deep breaths can help reset your system. Imagine filling your lungs like a balloon, hold for a few seconds, and then let it out slowly. Feel the diffcrence?

Next, grounding exercises are your new best friend. The "5-4-3-2-1" technique is a favorite. Identify five things you can see, four you can touch, three you can hear, two you can smell, and one you can taste. It's all about bringing you back to the present moment.

And don't forget about positive self-talk. Instead of letting that inner critic run wild, challenge those thoughts. Remind yourself of past successes and that everyone, at some point, feels a bit out of their depth.

Lastly, consider visualization. Before entering a social situation, picture it going well. Imagine yourself confident and relaxed.

Remember, these techniques are like muscles. The more you use them, the stronger they get. So, flex those calmness muscles and show social anxiety who's boss!

Growing Confidence in Larger Groups

Hey there, superstar! So, you've been working on managing that social anxiety, and now you're ready to dive into the deep end: larger groups. It might seem daunting, but with a few strategies up your sleeve, you'll be mingling like a pro in no time.

Firstly, let's start small. Before jumping into a big crowd, try joining smaller group settings and gradually increase the number of people. It's like testing the waters before taking the plunge.

Next, always remember the power of preparation. If you're attending an event or gathering, do a little homework. Know the agenda, familiarize yourself with the venue, or even prepare a few conversation starters. Being prepared can give you that extra boost of confidence.

Another tip? Find a buddy. Having a friend or colleague by your side can make navigating larger groups less intimidating. They can introduce you to others and help keep the conversation flowing.

Lastly, focus on listening. Often, we're so worried about what to say next that we forget the art of active listening. People appreciate a good listener, and it takes the pressure off you to constantly come up with things to say.

Sub-chapter 7.5: The Power of Non-Verbal Communication

Understanding Body Language Cues

Hey there, savvy communicator! Ever heard the saying, "Actions speak louder than words"? Well, in the world of non-verbal communication, that's spot on. Our body language often reveals more about our feelings and intentions than our words do. Let's dive into the fascinating realm of body language cues.

First off, the eyes. They're not just the windows to the soul; they're a billboard of our emotions. A steady gaze can show confidence, while avoiding eye contact might hint at discomfort or shyness.

Then there's the posture. Standing tall with shoulders back? That screams confidence. Slouching or hunching? It might convey insecurity or disinterest.

Our hands are chatterboxes too. Ever noticed someone fidgeting with their fingers during a tense meeting? Or how about those expansive hand gestures when someone's excited? Yep, hands spill the beans!

And let's not forget the feet. Pointing towards an exit might mean someone's itching to leave, while feet directed towards you can indicate genuine interest.

Our body language can convey a myriad of emotions, often without us even realizing it. So, the next time you're in a conversation, pay a little extra attention to those silent cues. They might just tell you more than words ever could!

Projecting Confidence Without Words

Hey, friend! Ever walked into a room and felt someone's presence before they even spoke? That's the magic of non-verbal confidence. Let's unravel how you can radiate that same self-assured energy, without uttering a single word.

First up, posture. Standing tall with a straight back isn't just good for your spine; it's a universal sign of confidence. Think of it as wearing an invisible crown. Own your space!

Next, the eye contact game. Locking eyes, even for a few seconds, can convey trust and assurance. It's like silently saying, "I see you, and I'm present in this moment."

Your hands can be powerful allies too. Instead of hiding them or fidgeting, use them to emphasize points or simply let them rest comfortably. It's all about being purposeful with your movements.

And don't forget those feet. Plant them firmly on the ground. It's a subtle way to show you're grounded and unshakable.

Even in the animal kingdom, non-verbal cues play a pivotal role in establishing dominance and trust. So, channel that inner lion or lioness. Let your body do the talking and show the world the confident superstar you truly are!

Reading and Responding to Others' Non-Verbal Signals

Hey there, savvy communicator! While we've chatted about how you can project confidence without words, let's flip the script. It's equally crucial to pick up on the silent cues others throw your way. Let's dive into this fascinating world of unspoken dialogue.

Imagine you're at a café, and someone across the table keeps glancing at the door. That's not just a random act; it's a sign they might be feeling anxious or eager to leave. Recognizing these cues can help you adjust the conversation or check in on their comfort.

Then there's the classic crossed arms. While it's easy to label this as a defensive stance, context is key. Maybe they're just cold! But if paired with a furrowed brow or distant gaze, it might be time to switch topics or lighten the mood.

Ever noticed someone's foot tapping rapidly? That could be impatience or nervousness knocking. Responding with a calming tone or a reassuring smile can work wonders.

Micro-expressions (brief facial changes) can reveal genuine emotions, even if someone's trying to hide them. So, keep those eyes peeled and ears tuned. By understanding and reacting to these silent signals, you're not just communicating; you're truly connecting.

Chapter Nine

Celebrating Small Wins

The Incremental Path to Overall Confidence

"Success is the sum of small efforts, repeated day in and day out." – Robert Collier

In the grand tapestry of life, it's easy to become fixated on the large, defining moments. However, true confidence isn't just built in leaps and bounds; it's also crafted in the tiny, seemingly inconsequential steps we take daily. This chapter shines a light on the magic of small victories, emphasizing how each minor achievement paves the way for overall confidence. Just as a mosaic is made up of individual tiles, our confidence is the culmination of numerous small wins we often overlook.

By recognizing and celebrating these moments, we not only boost our self-esteem but also reinforce a positive feedback loop, encouraging more such wins. It's about cherishing the journey as much as the destination, understanding that every step, no matter how small, is a move in the right direction. So, let's embark on this enlightening journey, learning to give ourselves credit for the little things, and in doing so, building a robust foundation of unwavering confidence.

Sub-chapter 8.1: The Power of Micro-Achievements

Recognizing Daily Triumphs

Hey there, fellow journeyer through life! Let's chat about something we often overlook: our daily triumphs. You know, those little moments that might seem insignificant but are actually mini victories? Like finally clearing out that daunting email backlog, or choosing a salad over fries (even though those fries were calling your name). These moments might not make headlines, but they're the unsung heroes of our confidence-building journey.

Every day, amidst the hustle and bustle, we achieve things that deserve a pat on the back. Maybe you held your ground in a tricky conversation, or perhaps you finally nailed that yoga pose you've been working on. These achievements, no matter how small, are testament to your growth and resilience.

Dr. Robert Brooks, a renowned psychologist, once said, "Small successes lead to bigger successes." And he's spot on! By acknowledging these daily triumphs, we not only boost our mood but also lay the groundwork for bigger achievements.

So, let's make it a habit. At the end of each day, take a moment to reflect on your mini-victories. Celebrate them, cherish them, and let them be the stepping stones to your ever-growing confidence.

The Ripple Effect of Small Successes

Alright, let's dive into a beautiful phenomenon: the ripple effect of our small wins. Picture this: you toss a pebble into a still pond. That tiny pebble creates ripples that expand far beyond its initial impact, right? Similarly, our little achievements, no matter how modest they seem, can set off a chain reaction of positivity in our lives.

Think about the last time you accomplished a small task you'd been putting off. Maybe you finally organized your workspace or took a short walk during lunch. That sense of accomplishment didn't just stop there, did it? It probably gave you a boost of energy, a spring in your step, and suddenly, tackling the next task didn't seem so daunting.

James Clear, the author of "", mentions, "Habits are the compound interest of self-improvement." This means that each small success not only adds to our confidence bank but also compounds over time, leading to significant growth.

So, the next time you achieve something small, remember: it's not just a drop in the ocean. It's the start of a wave, a momentum builder. And as these waves come together, they form a powerful tide pushing you towards greater confidence and achievement.

Journaling to Track Progress

Let's chat about a simple yet transformative tool: journaling. Now, I'm not talking about the "Dear Diary" entries from our childhood, but rather a focused way to track our daily achievements and growth.

Imagine ending each day by jotting down your small wins. It could be as simple as speaking up in a meeting, trying a new recipe, or even just taking a moment for yourself amidst a hectic day. Over time, flipping through these pages becomes a journey through your personal growth story.

According to a study by the University of Rochester, journaling can help individuals prioritize problems, fears, and concerns. By tracking our micro-achievements, we're not just listing tasks; we're acknowledging our efforts, no matter how small. This act of recognition reinforces our self-worth and motivates us to chase bigger goals.

Moreover, on days when self-doubt creeps in (and let's face it, we all have those days), revisiting these journals serves as a tangible reminder of how far we've come. It's like having a personal cheerleader in book form!

So, consider keeping a journal by your bedside. A few minutes each night can pave the way for a more confident and self-aware you.

Sub-chapter 8.2: Creating a Reward System

Reinforcing Positive Behaviors

Hey there, let's dive into a fun topic: rewards! Remember those gold stars we used to get in school for a job well done? Turns out, they were onto something. Reinforcing positive behaviors isn't just for kids; it's a powerful tool for adults too.

When we reward ourselves for making good choices or achieving goals, we're essentially giving our brain a little pat on the back. It's like telling our inner self, "Hey, you did great, and you deserve this treat!" This positive reinforcement strengthens our motivation and encourages us to keep pushing forward.

According to Dr. James Clear, author of "Atomic Habits", immediate rewards make a behavior more attractive, which in turn increases the odds of repeating it in the future. So, whether it's indulging in your favorite dessert after a week of consistent workouts or buying that book you've been eyeing after completing a challenging project, these rewards serve as a reminder of your hard work.

The key is to choose rewards that resonate with you personally. It's all about celebrating your journey and the steps you take along the way. So, next time you achieve something, big or small, give yourself a well-deserved treat. You've earned it!

Setting Up Tangible and Intangible Rewards

Alright, let's chat about rewards! When we think of rewards, often our minds jump straight to tangible goodies like a new pair of shoes or a delicious slice of cake. And while these are fantastic (who doesn't love cake?), there's a whole world of intangible rewards out there that can be just as fulfilling.

Tangible rewards are the physical things we can touch and see. Think of them as the "I can hold this in my hand" kind of rewards. Maybe it's that book you've been wanting to read, or perhaps a spa day after a month of hard work.

On the flip side, intangible rewards are the feel-good, non-materialistic kind. These could be things like taking a day off to relax, spending quality time with loved ones, or even just allowing yourself an afternoon nap. Experiences, an intangible reward, can lead to longer-lasting happiness than material purchases.

The beauty of rewards is that they're personal. What works for one person might not work for another. So, mix and match! Find the balance between tangible and intangible that feels right for you. Remember, it's all about celebrating your achievements in a way that feels meaningful.

Avoiding Pitfalls Like Over-Rewarding

Hey there, let's dive into a little chat about rewards. Now, while it's super fun to treat ourselves (because who doesn't love a good pat on the back?), there's a sneaky side to rewards we need to be wary of: over-rewarding.

Imagine running a mile and then thinking, "I did great! I deserve a whole chocolate cake." Sounds tempting, right? But here's the catch: if we constantly over-reward our achievements, we might end up negating the very progress we're trying to celebrate. It's like taking one step forward and two steps back.

According to Dr. Jane Nelsen, an expert in, over-rewarding can also diminish our internal motivation. If we're always looking for that external treat, we might forget the joy and satisfaction that comes from the achievement itself.

So, what's the game plan? Moderation is key. It's essential to find a balance. Celebrate your wins, absolutely! But ensure the reward matches the effort. And sometimes, the best reward is recognizing how far you've come and the growth you've experienced.

In the end, it's all about creating a reward system that uplifts and motivates you, without going overboard. Keep it balanced, and you'll be golden!

Sub-chapter 8.3: Continuous Learning and Growth

Adopting a Lifelong Learner Mindset

Hey there, friend! Let's chat about something that's a real game-changer: adopting a lifelong learner mindset. You know, it's that spark that keeps some folks forever curious, always hungry to know more. It's not just about acing exams or getting degrees; it's about embracing the joy of learning in every phase of life.

Imagine seeing the world as a vast library, where every experience, every conversation, and even every mistake is a lesson waiting to be absorbed. Cool, right? This mindset doesn't just keep your brain sharp; it makes life richer and more colorful.

Carol Dweck, a renowned psychologist, talks about the "" in her work. She believes that abilities can be developed through dedication and hard work. This perspective aligns perfectly with being a lifelong learner. It's about believing that you can grow, change, and evolve, no matter your age or stage in life.

So, next time you're faced with something new or challenging, lean into it. Be that person who asks questions, seeks answers, and relishes the journey of discovery. After all, life's too short to ever stop learning!

Expanding One's Knowledge Base

Hey there! Let's dive into a topic that's close to my heart: expanding our knowledge base. Think of your mind as this vast, beautiful garden. Now, what if you could plant new seeds of knowledge in it every day? Sounds exciting, right?

In today's digital age, we're incredibly lucky. The world's information is literally at our fingertips. From online courses, and podcasts, to good old-fashioned books, there's a treasure trove of knowledge waiting to be explored. Remember that documentary on space you stumbled upon? Or that cooking class you took on a whim? Each of these experiences adds a new layer to your understanding of the world.

Bill Gates, one of the world's most successful entrepreneurs, is known for his voracious reading habits. He believes that reading and learning from different fields can spark innovation and new ideas. Here's the.

But here's the thing: expanding your knowledge isn't just about accumulating facts. It's about connecting the dots, seeing patterns, and gaining a deeper understanding of the world around you. So, the next time you're curious about something, dive in! Explore, learn, and grow. Your mind's garden will thank you for it.

Finding Joy in the Journey

Hey, friend! Let's chat about something we often overlook: the sheer joy of the learning journey. You see, it's easy to get caught up in the end goals, the certificates, the accolades. But have you ever paused to relish the moments in between?

Imagine you're learning to play the guitar. Sure, mastering a song feels fantastic, but there's something uniquely beautiful about those initial awkward chord transitions, the first time you strum without thinking, or the laughter when you mess up a note. It's in these moments that the magic truly happens.

Author Robert Louis Stevenson once said, "To travel hopefully is a better thing than to arrive." And he's spot on! The journey, with its ups and downs, challenges and triumphs, is where we truly grow. It's where we discover more about ourselves, our passions, and the world around us.

So, the next time you embark on a new learning adventure, remember to savor each step. Find joy in the little victories, the stumbles, and even the detours. Because, at the end of the day, it's not just about reaching the destination, but cherishing the beautiful journey that takes you there.

Sub-chapter 8.4: Overcoming Plateaus

Recognizing Signs of Stagnation

Hey there! Let's dive into a topic we've all faced but rarely talked about hitting a plateau. You know, that feeling when you're stuck in a rut, and everything seems a bit... "meh"? It's like you're jogging in place, not really moving forward. But how do you know for sure you've hit this stagnant phase?

First off, you might notice a lack of enthusiasm for things you once loved. That book you were writing or that course you were acing suddenly feels like a chore. Then there's the feeling of being on autopilot, just going through the motions without any real zest.

Another sign? You're not seeing progress. Maybe you've been at the same skill level in your hobby for a while, or your career hasn't advanced despite your efforts. And let's not forget that nagging feeling of dissatisfaction, even if you can't quite put your finger on why.

But here's the silver lining: recognizing stagnation is the first step to breaking free from it. As the wise saying goes, "The first step to solving a problem is recognizing there is one." So, if any of this sounds familiar, take heart. You're already on your way to reigniting that spark and moving past the plateau.

Re-strategizing for Continued Progress

Alright, so you've identified that you're at a bit of a standstill. No sweat! Every champion, every expert, every person who's ever achieved something great has been there. The key isn't to avoid these plateaus but to learn how to dance around them. Let's chat about re-strategizing to keep that progress train chugging.

First, take a step back and assess. What's been working? What hasn't? Sometimes, we're so deep in the process that we can't see the forest for the trees. A fresh perspective can do wonders.

Next, shake things up a bit. If you've been doing the same routine or using the same approach, it might be time for a change. Remember, insanity is doing the same thing over and over and expecting different results. So, try a new tactic, learn a different method, or even consult someone who's been where you are.

Lastly, set mini-goals. Instead of aiming for that big, daunting target, break it down into smaller, more manageable chunks. Celebrate each little victory, and use it as fuel to propel you to the next.

Remember, plateaus are just temporary pauses, not full stops. With a bit of re-strategizing, you'll be back on your upward trajectory in no time!

Seeking Mentorship and Guidance

Hey there, champ! So, you've hit a bit of a rough patch, huh? It happens to the best of us. But here's a little secret: you don't have to navigate it alone. Ever thought about seeking out a mentor? Let's dive into why this might be the game-changer you need.

Imagine having someone in your corner who's been through the same challenges, faced the same doubts, and overcame them. That's what a mentor brings to the table. They're like your personal GPS, helping you navigate the tricky terrains of life.

Now, you might be thinking, "Where do I even find a mentor?" Great question! Start by looking around in your community or workplace. There are often experienced individuals eager to share their wisdom. Websites like LinkedIn can also be goldmines for connecting with potential mentors in your field.

But remember, mentorship isn't just a one-way street. It's a partnership. Be open, be curious, and be ready to invest time into the relationship. Listen actively, ask questions, and apply their guidance.

In the words of Isaac Newton, "If I have seen further, it is by standing on the shoulders of giants." So, why not find your giant and see how much further you can go?

Sub-chapter 8.5: Future Visioning and Goal Setting

Crafting a Vision Board

Have you ever felt like your goals are just floating around in your head, feeling a bit intangible? Let's bring them to life with a vision board. It's like giving your dreams a visual address, and trust me, it's a whole lot of fun!

A vision board is essentially a collage of images, quotes, and reminders of your aspirations. Think of it as your personal mood board for life. The magic lies in its ability to make your dreams feel more 'real' and attainable.

Starting one is simple. Grab a board or even just a piece of cardboard. Now, think about what you want to achieve. Maybe it's a dream vacation, a career goal, or a personal milestone. Flip through magazines, print pictures, or even doodle – whatever resonates with your dreams.

Place them on your board in a way that feels right to you. There's no 'one-size-fits-all' here. It's YOUR vision, after all. Once done, place your board somewhere you'll see it daily.

As the famous saying goes, "What you focus on grows." By constantly visualizing your goals, you're setting yourself up for success. So, ready to give your dreams a home? Let's get crafting!

Setting Short-Term and Long-Term Goals

Hey there, goal-setter! Let's chat about the art of setting goals. You see, goals are like destinations on a roadmap. Some are just around the corner, while others are miles away. But each one is essential in guiding our journey.

Short-term goals are those "around the corner" targets. Think of them as stepping stones. They're achievable in a few weeks or months and give you that quick satisfaction. Want to start a morning routine? Or maybe save up for that trendy gadget? These are your short-term goals. They're crucial because they build momentum and keep you motivated.

On the flip side, we have long-term goals. These are your "miles away" dreams, the ones that require time, patience, and consistent effort. Maybe it's buying a house, achieving a significant career milestone, or traveling the world. They might seem daunting, but remember, every marathon starts with a single step.

The trick is to balance both. Your short-term goals can act as milestones on the way to your long-term dreams. Celebrate each achievement, no matter how small, and keep your eyes on the prize.

Embracing the Journey with Optimism and Vigor

Hey there, fellow traveler! Let's talk about the journey we're all on. You know, life's unpredictable roller coaster filled with ups, downs, twists, and turns. But here's the thing: it's not just about the destination; it's about how we ride.

Optimism is like that trusty backpack filled with essentials. It lightens our steps, even when the path gets rocky. It's the belief that no matter how cloudy the day, the sun is shining somewhere behind those clouds. And guess what? This sunny outlook isn't just a feel-good mantra; studies have shown that optimists tend to live longer, healthier lives!

Now, let's talk vigor. It's the energy, the zest, the enthusiasm we bring to our daily tasks. It's waking up and saying, "Today's a brand-new day, and I'm going to make the most of it!" It's about diving into challenges head-first, with a smile on our faces and a spring in our step.

So, as we set our goals and envision our future, let's promise ourselves this: We won't just focus on the endgame. We'll cherish every moment, every lesson, every setback, and every win. Because, in the grand tapestry of life, every thread counts.

As the saying goes, "Life is a journey, not a destination." So, lace up those shoes, and let's hit the road with optimism and vigor!

www.ingramcontent.com/pod-product-compliance
Lightning Source LLC
Chambersburg PA
CBHW060817050426
42449CB00008B/1694